What People
CHANG

I've seen this Change Expert Sp... ... ... has a way of making you feel as though you are sitting at your kitchen table with him. Now, in this same way, his book weaves his stories of Changercise into powerful and usable techniques for both your professional and personal growth. Read it Now!

> —*Arnold Sanow, Professional Speaker, author of 6 books*
> including *"Present with Power, Punch and Pizzazz."*

• • •

If you're struggling with change in your life and think one more book can't possibly make a difference, think again. This change expert has the rare gift of breaking things down (both at the podium and now in printed form) into bite-sized pieces that you can use to change yourself on a daily basis in your work, home, and play.

> —*Gregory Shanahan, Manager* at American Capital

• • •

At last, a real book about change that is practical and not theoretical— written by a Change Expert Speaker who knows what he is talking about.

> —*John Bailey, Entrepreneur, Global Speaker—"Building Leadership*
> *Culture", John Bailey Communications*

• • •

Whether you want to make a minor change or a major one— "Changercise—Change Your Thinking → Change Your Results" is a ***must have!***

> —*Patsy Anderson, Concept Designer, PWN Radio, Women's*
> *Expo Forum*

• • •

This is the ultimate change reference guide and handbook. Anyone who ever needs to make any type of change should refer to it often.

> —*Matt Fee, Regional Accounts Manager* at Reed Elsevier

• • •

This book is jam-packed with real-life, how-to information that can be used instantly.

> —*Pamela Hetherington, Artist, Choreographer and Dance Educator,*
> *Take It Away, Inc.*

• • •

DW has been a great mentor to me since I met him a year ago. His book has changed my life and the way I approach life.

—Jagadesh Mohanram, CEO, Aragorn Systems

∎   ∎   ∎

His speaking style is now in print—Everyone who is really serious about making a change in their work or personal life should get this speakers' book. It's packed with clear, concise ideas and techniques that can be used immediately. A must read for those who want to make change Now!

—Andrew Finn, Professor, George Mason University, radio talk show host, professional keynote speaker

∎   ∎   ∎

I loved your testimonials from your many clients. It is clear that these techniques work well.

—Sue Hodgson, Senior Editor at CRC Press, London Office

∎   ∎   ∎

This is a practical no-nonsense guide to what really works in making changes successfully.

—Patrick Haggerty, President, Haggerty Group, Keynote speaker, Grassroots Legislative Advocacy

∎   ∎   ∎

Great advice from a professional who knows what it takes to "make change a friendly word again." You'll do well to have the author as your mentor as you use this resource to chart your new path to positive change.

—Maria Rock, CEO/Founder, Photographer and Educator at Maria Rock Photography

∎   ∎   ∎

This Change-Expert Speaker has put his wisdom in print. Well done, DW.

—Eric Kelley, Logistician, Professional Speaker, U.S. Government

∎   ∎   ∎

If you want to improve the direction toward your goals with immediate practical information that will ***cut your learning curve by 90%*** this book is for you.

—Randall Taussig, CEO/Founder, Blue Core Leadership, Coaching/Training Entrepreneurial Organizations

Changercise

Change Your Thinking → Change Your Results

DW Starr

iUniverse LLC
Bloomington

CHANGERCISE
Change Your Thinking → Change Your Results

iUniverse books may be ordered through booksellers or by contacting:

iUniverse LLC
1663 Liberty Drive
Bloomington, IN 47403
www.iuniverse.com
1-800-Authors (1-800-288-4677)

ISBN: 978-1-4917-1621-2 (sc)
ISBN: 978-1-4917-1622-9 (e)

Library of Congress Control Number: 2013922296

Printed in the United States of America.

iUniverse rev. date: 01/14/2014

I want to thank three people who have been instrumental in my success as a husband, father, change-expert speaker, radio show host, and sales and executive coach.

To my wife of more than twenty years, Liz—thanks for your love, patience, and support.

To my son, Mark—thanks for keeping my creative juices flowing.

To my son, Seth—thanks for keeping my mind at its peak.

I also want to thank all my speaking engagement and executive coaching clients over the years who have let me experiment with them as I created *Changercise*. I couldn't have done it without you.

I especially want to thank the following clients who were willing to share their changercise testimonials:

Catherine V.
Tina O.
Tommy H.
Garrett B.
Josephine H.
Maryanne D.

You have convinced me that it is time for individuals, companies, and organizations around the world to know the value of changercise and how it will help them create a more successful future.

Contents

Introduction

Change is the essence of life. Be willing to surrender who you are for who you will become.

Changercise is about changing the way you think and thinking the way to change.

Changercise is, as you would suspect, the combination of the two words *change* and *exercise*.

Changercise is made up of six specific *change exercises* that I developed over thirteen years of working with individuals, companies, and associations. I helped them to embrace, adapt to, and manage change in the workplace successfully—through speaking, training, and executive coaching.

I've included testimonials from six of my clients who have used these changercises in their own lives to give you an idea of how they have helped them, both professionally and personally.

You'll read about these and others:

- *Catherine*, a frontline supervisor, with the help of this changercise, found a way to be calmer and have more energy at the same time.

- *Tina*, the CEO of one of the biggest clothing chains in the world, always struggled with her weight—until using this changercise.

- *Tommy*, now the division head of a Fortune 500 company, learned with this changercise to put the employment disappointments of his past behind him in order to reach that position.

- *Garrett*, a sales team leader, applied this changercise to effectively deal with three belligerent customers in a row—without bringing the frustration home with him.

- *Josephine*, a pediatrician, found herself crying on December 23 but then used this changercise to bring joy to her life and to the lives of countless others.

- *Maryanne*, a corporate secretary for a large bank, decided she wanted to move up the ladder into management and used this changercise to help achieve her goal.

I've been working with CEOs, CFOs, production managers, division chiefs, department heads, sales managers and trainers, government agencies, commercial and social associations of various types, the US Army, life coaches, and many other groups with one thing in mind . . . assisting them to *change the way they think and think the way to change.*

Here's your chance to do the same.

You now have in your hands the opportunity to do *three things for yourself. Changercise* will inform, entertain, and galvanize you to action.

Einstein said, "Everything should be made as simple as possible, but not simpler."

The definition of *belief* in dictionary.com is "confidence in the truth or existence of something not immediately susceptible to rigorous proof."

My goal for you is to have *Changercise* be your simple solution. And to have the *belief* it will work for you.

Many great books have been written about change, with different approaches. Unlike many of them, *Changercise* is written for reader participation. You can consider it your *participation invitation* to a changed future full of growth and adventure.

Let's get started with that growth and adventure right now . . .

Think for a moment. Why did you decide to read *Changercise*? What did you hope to achieve or learn? Write down your three-sentence goal here:

Great! As you probably know, without definiteness of purpose, your results will be hazy and unclear. Okay, now that you know what your focus is for reading *Changercise,* you can move forward.

As the title suggests, *Changercise* is about *you* exercising the change you need and want in your life and/or workplace. You can start reading it on a daily basis. Each day will build upon the previous day. Each week will build upon the previous. And yes, each month will build upon the previous.

For as anyone who has run a business, lost weight, done a 5K run, managed a sales force, received a college degree, or raised a child knows, success is not a one-time effort or a flash in the pan, and it can't be figured out in a day or even a month.

It is a way of viewing the world and taking action on that viewpoint on a daily, weekly, and monthly basis. And it is your attitude toward that goal that creates the change followed by your consistent actions.

I started this chapter with this statement:

Change is the essence of life. Be willing to surrender who you are for who you will become.

Change is a constant, whether we like it or not. And if you indeed want to make a major change in your business or personal life, you need to be willing to let go of the old, to embrace the *new* and forthcoming. A good way to let go of the "old way of doing or being" is to first recognize what need it was filling. Once you do that, you'll then be able to embrace the *new* more comfortably. I'll be giving you examples of how to do this throughout *Changercise*.

I know that no two people are alike. You all have your idiosyncrasies and your unique belief systems. So I am not asking you to be something you are not. *I am asking you to become who you are meant to be.* We only have so much time on this earth . . . remember, your clock is ticking.

Here's a preview of what's coming in chapter 3 . . .

Speaking with many of my clients through the years, three facts have emerged related to this particular changercise.

1. No matter how negative the results of being in your ouch zone (OZ) might be, you still find positive pieces in your own personal OZs—pieces that fill a need of some kind.

2. You are a creature of habit, and it is often easier to just keep doing what you've always done, whether that is driving the same route to work or holding on to pain and suffering with it.

3. For my clients who are willing to suspend disbelief, to do the hard work of change, this changercise catapults you months and sometimes years ahead of where you would be without it. Faith is a powerful catalyst for change.

This changercise *is for you when you have decided it's time to move on!* Only you will decide the appropriate time. But all too often you know you *should* but *can't*. This changercise is designed to help those of you who *can't*.

So that's just a little taste of what you can look forward to, but for now . . .

Changercise is designed to be your living change manual. Although each of the five changercises plus bonus is independent of the others, when used together, they create exponential change. *Changercise* is meant to be used in many ways. You read it like any other book, page by page or chapter by chapter. You can skip to a favorite chapter, or for some of you, the final chapter. You can skim the italicized words to get the gist. You can only do the assignments at the end of each chapter. *It's your choice.*

Changercise is a way for you to actively participate—both physically and mentally—in creating your more successful future.

I hope and believe that this is at least part of why you are reading this in the first place.

You want to change the direction of something in your life, be it business, job, social, psychological, financial, emotional, spiritual, physical, or *all of these.*

Changercise takes you on a *virtual journey* through the files in your mental computer. And not only do you travel, you get to text yourself messages as you go along. You'll also be in contact with friends both past and present in this extraordinary escapade. *Your life will become an ongoing adventure.*

Here's how *Changercise* is organized:
* description of the changercise
* benefits of the changercise
* how to do the changercise
* reading a client's changercise testimonial
* journaling your thoughts, feelings, and observations

Journaling will be on paper or electronically. Either way, it is critical to keep this record of your impressions and feelings. It will become instrumental in reaching your goals, both for reading *Changercise* and for your other short- and long-term goals, whether they are business, personal, or both.

Share your changercise with a friend. Each of you can do the changercise and you can communicate with each other about the questions and your answers. You can communicate by text, e-mail, or the old-fashioned way, by phone. I guarantee this will speed up your ability to apply this in your daily life and help you reach your three-sentence goal that much faster.

And then make sure you share it with us at www. changercise.com and keep us in your loop.

This is all about your choice to change.

Chapter 1
Silence Is Golden

Yes, this is the title of a song originally sung by the Four Seasons in 1964 and made popular on the rock scene in 1967 by the Tremolos.

I'm sure it was a great song for its time. This chapter is not about that song.

What is *Silence Is Golden*?
Silence Is Golden is the recognition of the power of silence in your life.

This changercise is all about mental relaxation, quieting your mind.

But wait, before you go any further. If you haven't done the first assignment in the introduction (*think for a moment—why did you decide to read* Changercise?), please turn back and do it. I'll wait while you do that . . . great! As you know, without definiteness of purpose, your results will be hazy and unclear. Okay, now that you know what your focus is in reading *Changercise*, you can move forward.

As I said in the introduction, changercise is made up of two words: change and exercise.

The main theme of *Changercise* is . . .

Change is the essence of life. Be willing to surrender who you are for who you will become.

This is all about
your choice to change.

Change is a constant, whether we like it or not. And if you indeed want to make a major change in your business or personal life, you need to be willing to let go of the old, to embrace the new and forthcoming. A good way to let go of the old way of doing or being is to first recognize what need it was filling. Once you do that, you'll then be able to embrace the new more comfortably. I'll be giving you examples of how to do this throughout *Changercise*, and you'll read testimonials of clients just like you who have used these changercises in both their business and personal lives. They've used them to change things about themselves they were not happy about, including their weight, lack of discipline, stress and anxiety, lack of confidence, anger, and more.

The definition of *belief* on dictionary.com is "confidence in the truth or existence of something not immediately susceptible to rigorous proof."

If you really work this book, you can expect to get results the first week . . . and every week thereafter. The results will vary based on your goals for reading *Changercise*, the time and effort you invest, and the *belief* it will work for you.

Again, here's a preview of what's coming in chapter 3 . . .

----

1. No matter how negative the results of being in your OZ might be, you still find positive pieces in your own personal ouch zones—pieces that fill a need of some kind.

2. You are a creature of habit, and it is often easier to just keep doing what you've always done, whether that is driving the same route to work or holding on to pain and suffering with it.

3. For my clients who are willing to suspend disbelief, to do the hard work of change, this changercise catapults you months and sometimes years ahead of where you would be without it. Faith is a powerful catalyst for change . . .

Before we continue with the first changercise, Silence Is Golden, I want you to create for yourself a baseline so you can monitor your growth while reading and doing these changercises.

I want you to answer the following sentences in this order:

Five years ago . . .
Who was I?

Who did I want to be?

Ten years ago . . .
Who was I?

Who did I want to be?

Fifteen years ago . . .
Who was I?

Who did I want to be?

In high school . . .
Who was I?

Who did I want to be?

As a ten-year-old . . .
Who was I?

Who did I want to be?

Today, here and now . . .
Who am I?

What was my vision of where I would be today?

What's different?

What works?

What doesn't?

What must change?

Today, here and now . . .
What have I done and been?

What do I feel great about?

Today, here and now . . .
What do I regret not doing?

What do I regret not being?

Today, here and now . . .
What do I want to do, even if I don't think I can?

What do I want to be, even if I don't think I can?

Today, here and now . . .
What would I do if I knew I couldn't fail?

What would I be if I knew I couldn't fail?

Who do you want to become?

How has that changed?

What's the dream now?

What must change?

What steps do you need to take today to change your direction?

That was hard work, wasn't it? You should be proud of yourself for digging deep to find these answers. Well done!

Okay, now let's continue with the first changercise.

Today, silence is a very valuable commodity.

Silence Is Golden is the recognition of the power of silence in your life.

Here is what some famous folks have had to say about silence:

I have often lamented that we cannot close our ears with as much ease as we can our eyes.—Richard Steele

Nowadays most men lead lives of noisy desperation. —James Thurber

All men's miseries derive from not being able to sit in a quiet room alone.—Blaise Pascal

True silence is the rest of the mind; it is to the spirit what sleep is to the body—nourishment and refreshment.— William Penn

Silence is the element in which great things fashion themselves.—Carlyle

Silence is a source of great strength.—Lao Tzu

Why do Silence Is Golden?

There are a myriad of reasons to do this changercise.

Mindfulness practice leads to increases in regional brain gray matter density.

Participating in an eight-week mindfulness meditation program appears to make measurable changes in brain regions associated with memory, sense of self, empathy, and stress. A team led by Massachusetts General Hospital (MGH) researchers reported that their study—published in *Psychiatry Research* (August 11, 2010) and supported by the National Institute of Health, the British Broadcasting Company, and the Mind and Life Institute—was the first to document meditation-produced changes over time in the brain's gray matter.

"Although the practice of meditation is associated with a sense of peacefulness and physical relaxation, practitioners have long claimed that meditation also provides cognitive and psychological benefits that persist throughout the day," says Sara Lazar, PhD, of the MGH Psychiatric Neuroimaging Research Program, the study's senior author. "This study demonstrates that changes in brain structure may underlie some of these reported improvements and that people are not just feeling better because they are spending time relaxing."

In a study done by the Mayo Clinic, published in *Explore* in 2009, subjects reported considerable lowering of stress and anxiety—and an increase of quality of life—after one month of silent meditation.

So with all the research on silence and meditation, of which I just noted two studies—and more in the references section—it seems quite obvious that silence *is* golden.

If there seems to be little room for silence, maybe that's because there is so much noise in your life today, everywhere you go.

According to the US Environmental Protection Agency's website, noise pollution adversely affects the lives of millions of people. Studies have shown that there are direct links between noise and health. Problems related to noise include stress-related illnesses, high blood pressure, speech interference, hearing loss, sleep disruption, and lost productivity. Noise Induced Hearing Loss (NIHL) is the most common and often discussed health effect, but research has shown that exposure to constant or high levels of noise can cause countless adverse health effects. Even low-level noise has been associated with increased aggression and other mental health problems, such as fibromyalgia, chronic fatigue syndrome, asthma, high blood pressure, alcoholism, menstrual disorders, multiple sclerosis, nicotine addiction, phobias, tremors, chronic pain, early menopause, stroke, immune system failure, sleep disorders, memory, concentration and learning disorders, cancer, gastrointestinal diseases, depression, post-traumatic stress syndrome, eczema, substance abuse, arthritis, psoriasis, migraines, diabetes, obesity, and anorexia.

With all the noise and its effects working against you, it's good to know you can do this first changercise and put some silence back into your life.

How do you do Silence Is Golden?

I want you to find a place that is void of sound. I am telling you now—this will not be easy.

You are surrounded by noise— in your office by the hum of computers; at the café by chatter; in your home by the air-conditioning fan and ticking clocks, or the sounds you put in your ears via TV, phones, and video games.

Our world and our lives are full of noise everywhere we turn, are they not?

Go to that place you found, sit still, and be in silence. I recommend you close your eyes. Now once you begin, if this situation is not totally silent, I want you to *stop*.

Do not do this changercise until you have complete silence.

Either find a new location or get something to block your hearing:

- cotton
- headphones
- earplugs
- wastebasket (That's a joke.)

Okay. I am going to assume you have now created a situation that is completely silent. Let's continue . . .

In the beginning this may be very difficult, especially if you are more comfortable with noise than quiet. You can start with three minutes. You can use the alarm on your watch, laptop, or cell phone. Close your eyes and sit in silence. Let your mind and thoughts travel where they will . . .

For some of you, you may want a more formal approach, such as meditation or contemplation. (Meditation or contemplation can be done in many ways. A list of types and techniques follows later in this chapter.) For now, we will focus on this very informal approach. So keep your eyes closed, and sit in silence.

For many of you, this will create a feeling and sensation you haven't felt for many years. And for some of you, you won't even be able to remember the last time you sat in silence.

Your goal is to sit as still as possible, not moving your body at all for those three minutes. The only movement should be your breathing. Your response to this changercise will be unique to your needs at that moment. Just let whatever happens happen. *Go with the flow,* as they say. For some of you, your heart may start to race. Some of you will feel tightness in your neck, back, or shoulders.

Some of you will develop an itch somewhere on your body. And you will have an overwhelming need to scratch it. *Wait, your three minutes will be up soon enough.* For others, you may get lightheaded or sleepy. For many, your thoughts will race from one topic to another, seemingly with no connection.

And others will have one thought that they seem to fixate on no matter how hard they try to change it. For some of you, your response won't be in this list. Any and all of these responses are normal.

Your goal, regardless of your response, is to sit as still as possible, not moving your body at all for those three minutes. The only movement should be your breathing. Again, for some of you, this will come rather easily. *But for many, these three minutes will seem like three hours.* Your thoughts and feelings tell you that this is a weird thing to do. It will irritate you. (We'll cover why you might be having that response later in this chapter.)

Hang in there—it gets easier the more you do it.

Did you find this easy or hard? If you found this to be easy, my guess is that you already do Silence Is Golden in your own way on a periodic basis. You have come to recognize the true value of silence.

For those of you who struggled a little or a lot with this, there is much to be gained and learned from this changercise.

As I said before, the goal is the *silence*, regardless of how you responded. Certain responses happen to almost everyone. My guess is that you, like me, are like most people, and one of these physical and mental responses happened to you as well.

Quieting distractions (heart racing). Did you notice that your heart was racing when you slowed down the distractions by sitting silently? Did you become aware of thoughts you might have otherwise ignored? Maybe you were anxious about something that came to the forefront of your mind with the quieting of distractions. It's an opportunity to pause and give more attention to what you need for yourself to be healthier and happier.

Becoming aware of pain (shoulder, head, neck pains). Pains are easier to ignore when you are focused on other thoughts and feelings. When we get quiet, they are easier to notice. These types of pains are often caused by stress in your environment. Look at what might be causing them. Work on eliminating or at least limiting them.

Learning not to react (an itch somewhere on your body). This is a good one. It's a true challenge to see if you can let go and not have to *react*, even though your immediate thought and even belief is that you must respond immediately by scratching it. Sitting quietly is often a good way to learn to *act* and not *react* to any given situation, whether it is with yourself or with other people.

Learning to relax (lightheaded or sleepy). You could be experiencing something called *relaxation*. All too often we can go days without relaxing—going and doing from one thing to the next without even a moment to pause in between. If you are always in a hurry and feel that sense of being overwhelmed, taking a moment to stop and be quiet could definitely cause you to have this kind of reaction.

Quieting your thoughts (thoughts racing and fixating). Is something on your mind? Are ideas flying by, in and out, at rapid speed? Are you fixating on a thought that you can't get out of your head, no matter what you try or do? Many of my clients say that they believe these effects are caused by never having enough time to bring them to a conclusion. Is your mind trying to tell you something? Are you listening?

Here are a few other places my clients have found a place to have silence, or at least a bit of quiet:

- Bathroom

- Basement

- Under the covers in your bed

- Your office

- A closet

- Unoccupied room or office

- Your car early in the morning in your driveway

- Your car in the parking lot before going into work

- Your car in the parking lot before going home from work

- Your car late at night in your driveway or garage

Journal where *your* quiet place is.

Here are some other forms of quiet time and meditation techniques you might want to try. You can find plenty of specific instruction on the Internet. A few of the sites you can go to are mayoclinic.com, zenhabits.net, mindful. org, synchronicity.org, tm.org, freemeditation.com, and many more.

Witnessing—Also known as objective viewing, witnessing is a meditation technique that will support you in developing a witness consciousness, which helps you develop the part of your mind that is able to observe thoughts and internal images as they arise and dissolve, without getting involved with them.

Prayer—Various religions practice different styles. We often think of prayer as speaking to God. This style encourages prayer as listening to God.

Breathing—Follow the rhythm of your breath in and out as you inhale and exhale. Your goal is to eventually be able to focus on your breathing to the exclusion of everything else in your external and internal environment.

Self-inquiry—This is the primary method through which self-realization, the realization of our true nature beyond mind and body, is achieved. You ask yourself, *Who's doing this thinking? Who is doing this feeling?*

Walking meditation—Walking meditation is a form of meditation of action, paying attention to body parts, breathing, heartbeat, your feet touching the ground, your motions, and your gravity.

Empty mind—Some consider this the most difficult meditation of all. Your goal is to have your thoughts disappear and have no new ones enter.

Transcendental meditation—This is chanting of a single word or phrase to achieve automatic self-transcending. It allows your mind to settle inward beyond thought to experience the source of thought—pure awareness.

Yoga—There are so many types. Some include meditation. Some of the yoga meditation types are sensation experience (mostly sense of touch or seeing), breath (many different methods), energy (chakras or channels of energy), attitudes (love, nonviolence, compassion), mantra (various types or traditions), visualized image (numerous varieties), and stream of thoughts (method known by different names).

Chakra meditation—This refers to seven energy points in the body and their clearing through meditation. The goal is to align the chakras in such a way as to achieve inner harmony and balance.

Healing meditation—Your goal is to connect the heart to the mind. Various methods are used: focusing (said to help with high blood pressure), protecting (dealing with negative people or thoughts around you), and flower balancing (helps the body's equilibrium, especially for nausea sufferers).

Guided meditation—This can be done by someone actually guiding you in person, listening to a recording of someone guiding you in a specific process, or listening to a music recording. While staying focused on the body—and in particular the muscles—the practitioner of guided meditation attempts to relax the muscles of the body. Allowing the body to completely relax allows the practitioner of guided meditation to then completely relax the mind.

Mindfulness—This is self-observation of thoughts without any interference, being in the here and now. Your goal is to achieve a mind that is stable and calm—and therefore feels content—recognizing that this is a natural aspect of the mind.

Journal how *you* chose to be quiet.

Each of the chapters in *Changercise* will provide a different client's testimonial.

This is the first one.

Catherine V.

I am a frontline supervisor at a freight delivery company. I find that I am often irritable and also tired more than I think is normal. My daughters tell me the same thing about my moods and energy. So when DW suggested this changercise might help me be less cranky and have more energy, I said to myself, "What do I have to lose? How hard can it be?"

I tried to find a place that was completely silent. I tried it at work and inside my house. It was too noisy in both places.

Then I tried sitting in my car in my garage with my earbuds in my ears without being plugged in. That was pretty darn quiet. So that is where I decided to do this changercise, early in the morning.

I thought about the last time I really had silence and I came up blank.

So here I was in the car. I decided I would try this for two minutes with my eyes closed, sitting as still as I possibly could. The first two times it was even hard for me to relax and sit still. I kept fidgeting. I tried to concentrate on just my breathing, since that seemed the simplest technique to start out with. It was so hard.

I found my thoughts about what was coming up that day flying around in my head. I didn't like doing it at all. I felt very constrained. I even remember feeling some kind of resentment.

I realized after the second time that if I was going to get anything out of this changercise, I would need to do it more often.

So the third week I did it twice that week. I still had trouble sitting still, but I was able to relax a bit more. By the fifth week I really had begun to notice a difference. I was more relaxed. I also had doubled the time to four minutes.

Now that might not seem like a big deal, but for me it was huge. Prior to this I couldn't even sit still for two minutes. I was slowly teaching myself how to relax, and I was also starting to look forward to what I labeled my quiet time.

By the end of the second month, something very strange happened. I was sitting in my car for about three minutes (by the way, I had built it up to five minutes), and I noticed my mind was relaxed. And then an answer to a problem I had been struggling with at work for two months just popped into my head. I wasn't even thinking about it. It just jumped in there out of nowhere.

I had heard from someone that I knew, who meditated on a regular basis, that she would sometimes have that happen. But it happened to me. I got so excited.

I am at a point now, after six months, I do my quiet time three to four times a week in the morning for ten minutes and one or two times a week in the evening for ten minutes. My goal in three months from now is to bump the time to fifteen minutes each time I sit quiet.

I can't begin to tell you how much calmer I feel and surprisingly at the same time have more energy during the day. My daughters told me they see a difference in how I am treating them. I am getting so much more accomplished at my job. My boss has even noticed it.

I would definitely suggest you try this changercise, even if you don't think you have time for it. It's definitely worth it, even if you shorten the time at first.

Let's look at a couple of things Catherine V. learned about change.

She learned that just like most things in life, success comes gradually. She was careful to set realistic time frame goals. She didn't try to sit silently for thirty minutes at a time. And even after nine months, her goals are still gradual and realistic for fifteen minutes at each sitting. She quickly realized the importance of regular and scheduled times. Consistency was very important for her routine.

She also learned that the technique itself helped her to change from being irritable and tired to calmer and having more energy. Now who wouldn't want more of those?

One of my former clients likes to sum it up with a paragraph she memorized in college:

"Best of all, silence is more energizing than a double latte, cheaper than a can of Red Bull, and more available than any fuel supply on the planet. The energy of silence always waits patiently, telling you, 'I am here when you need me. Be still and let me fuel you up. I am ready when you are.'"

I want you to think about a day last week that was very hectic, frustrating, boring, or anything else that caused you stress and anxiety.

Imagine for a moment, if right during that time, that you had told yourself it would be okay. That soon enough, you would be letting those feelings and thoughts wash away or clarify themselves because you would be sitting silently and having your *quiet time*.

How does that sound to you? Would just knowing you would have that to look forward to relieve some stress and anxiety?

Clients' comments about this changercise:

- "Taking a daily dose of quiet time for me helps me get through the day a calmer human being."
- "My doctor says that since I've been doing my silence technique, my blood pressure has gone down twenty points. Yay!"
- "Since doing this changercise for six months, I now have solutions to work problems, sometimes just popping into my head. I give it two thumbs up. It's quite amazing."

It's time to figure out what you learned and how you can apply it to your daily/weekly/monthly work and personal life and share with other readers or your friends if you choose.

Either by using paper or your favorite electronic device, journaling these answers will help you reach your original three-sentence goal you jotted down at the very beginning of this process, in the introduction. Write out the answer to each question with thoughtful consideration.

1. Where was the quietest place for you to do this changercise (home, work, car, other)?

2. How did the changercise help you be more calm or alert (or both) at work and at play?

3. What specific style of quiet time did you use? Did you try a few different ones until you found one you liked the most?

4. How would you use this changercise to take action on a specific situation you need to change?

Share your changercise with a friend. Each of you can do the changercise and then communicate with each other about the questions and your answers. You can communicate by text, e-mail, or the old-fashioned way, by phone. I guarantee you this will speed up your ability to apply this in your daily life and help you reach your three-sentence goal that much faster.

And then make sure you share it with us at www. changercise.com and keep us in your loop.

This is all about
your choice to change.

Chapter 2
Be a Time Traveler

What is *Be a Time Traveler*?

A time traveler can mean many things to many people. (We will leave the cosmic, metaphysical meaning for another time . . . perhaps another book.) What I mean here is *to be one who travels mentally back in time*. To go back to a time when you first had an inkling (yes, I said inkling) for the need and/or want to change.

I find for most people that this will be either very enjoyable or very difficult. Very few people are in the middle on this one.

Why Be a Time Traveler?

The goal of this changercise is for you to uncover some of the patterns that seem to *rule your life now.*

How long has it been since you thought about changing? Has it been six months, a year, three years, or maybe even ten or twenty? Maybe it's written down on a napkin or slip of paper. Or are you more organized and you have it written down in a journal or diary? Is it vague or very specific? Maybe it was connected to a certain person or an event in your life. It could have been a fleeting thought or idea.

Did you see something on the Internet, a YouTube video, or a news report that triggered it? Maybe you were watching TV or listening to the radio, and it crossed your mind. It could have been because of something a friend or relative said. Whatever the trigger was, it is personal.

Take a moment and write down those thoughts and feelings you had at a moment in the past when you thought about changing.

Now that you wrote it down, or texted it to a friend, you can refer back to it later in this chapter.

What is important here, today, is what you did about it.

Did you take action or bury it for another day? My goal for you is to dig it up and rekindle the flame!

The reasons for this changercise are as varied as there are people on the planet. Let's take a look at a couple of those reasons.

Our past can be a place of great joy, sadness, or both.

For some of us, our past is unbearable. When we look back there all we see is darkness, and so we immediately either hide from it or run away from it, mostly out of the pain we felt when we were originally in it. For others of us, it is not darkness; it is a void. Because of the sheer agony we felt then, we have completely obliterated any trace of it. It's as if it never even existed.

For many of us, it is as if our past has a split personality. One minute there are the awful things that happened, and the next moment there are the joys we remember. And for a few of us—a rather small few it seems—there are only pleasant and happy memories of days gone by.

So do you know where you fit in this set of descriptions?

Journal which description fits you.

Either way, to be a time traveler has its rewards.

The past is a real part of who we are, and a bit of a better understanding of it will shed light on our current selves. I've heard it said, "We are children, just in adult bodies." So examining how we reacted and responded to situations and people back then can provide a clearer path for growth today.

Looking back at what we did and why we did it is all about figuring out how to do it better, more easily, with less stress, and with more joy this time around.

Here are some examples of changes people often want to make and the potential moments in time that their bubbling up of the need or want for change occurred:

Lose weight—*I can't fit into that party dress anymore; another night wasted.*

Get married—*She is on my mind constantly, day and night, work and play.*

Get divorced—*My spouse is no longer interested in listening to me, period.*

Ask for a raise—*It's time I am more appreciated around here.*

Quit your job—*No matter what I do, it never seems good enough.*

Have a baby—*It's time for us to share our love with a child.*

Stop smoking—*I'm tired of freezing, standing outside the office building in the winter with strangers.*

Stop drinking—*I can't remember what I said last night, and why he now hates me.*

Exercise more often—*The elevator is broken one day and I feel like I might have a stroke.*

Start a hobby—*Work, work, work and then more work, work . . . I'm going brain-dead.*

Stand up and speak—*That was the idea I had three days ago, and she gets the credit because she stood up and spoke while I kept quiet.*

Take a class—*Wow, I bet I would be good at . . . if I only knew how to . . .*

Teach a class—*Okay, that's the third person today who said, "You should teach that."*

Face a fear—*You know it's time I stop giving in to this monster. How bad can it be?*

Get your teeth fixed—*I look like that guy from that old TV show,* The Beverly Hillbillies.

Start a new business—*I've got to do something; it's the only way I'll get out from underneath this debt.*

Learn a new language—*She's so beautiful. If only I could speak her language.*

Write a book—*How many years have I said, "You know, I could write a book about that!"*

Shoot a YouTube video—*My friends have got to see this. They'll never believe it unless I show them.*

Sing at a karaoke club—*Look, if Mary can do this, why can't I? It's time I face my fear.*

Okay, so I think by now you have the idea of what we are talking about and what you need to do.

Journal a time and situation when you wanted to change.

How do you be a time traveler?

You will find a quiet place, preferably the same location (see chapter 1).

And this time, unlike the method of the first chapter, you will have a very clear objective. You will travel back in time in your mind to that exact moment you began contemplating a change.

Go to that location where you have silence and close your eyes. Now travel back to the last time you wanted to change and take action.

Once you've got it, stay with it. Let's use our five senses now. First and foremost, use your strongest sense.

Let me digress for a moment. Years of research have shown that we all have a dominant sense. The three most common dominant senses are visual, auditory, and feeling (as in gut feelings). This is usually self-evident in how you sense the world. Often it is revealed in the words you choose to speak.

When you do something as simple as read a menu, which one of these responses is more likely yours? (Visual) *Number six looks great, I'll have that.* (Auditory) *Number six sounds great, I'll have that.* (Sensory) *I really feel like having number six tonight.* One response is no better or more correct than another. So if you don't already know your dominant sense, start paying close attention to how you speak and connect with your world around you. You may be amazed at what you learn!

Here are three quick examples of how your strongest sense would connect you to the time you decided you needed or wanted to change.

Sensory—You think back and the first inkling is how fat you *felt* when you were ten years old in the jeans your mother bought you. You could barely breathe, and you *felt* ugly. You wanted to lose that weight, so badly, right then and there. Now you're seventy-five pounds heavier than you want to be and you *feel* badly about yourself.

Visual—You can *see* an image in your mind's eye of a storefront with a *going out of business* sign on the front door. It's an image that seems to *show up* whenever you get a creative idea for a new business venture.

Auditory—You can *hear* the police siren in your head everywhere you drive. The last time you got a speeding ticket was going to be your last . . . so you thought. Ten years later and ten tickets later, you still *hear* it from time to time.

So now, let's get back to the changercise. For purposes of this example, we will use the sense of vision as your dominant one. And let's use *speaking up* as our goal example.

You would sit quietly and travel back in time to the last time you wanted to speak up and you didn't. Maybe you were at a business meeting six months ago?

You would *picture* the event. You would get very specific in your visualization. You would focus on what people's faces looked like. Remember their expressions. Were they bored or enthusiastic? Were they enjoying the business meeting, or were they looking at their cell phones, texting underneath the table? What was the color of the walls? Who exactly was in the room? Did anyone decide to speak up that day, or was it just the boss doing all of the talking, explaining and educating?

Was the room bright and sunny, or were the shades drawn and the room dull and gloomy? Was there art on the walls or were they barren? Was there food? Were there coffee cups and water glasses on the table?

The more detail, the better your memory will be triggered. Okay, so . . .

What did you want to say? Why didn't you? Were you afraid of making a mistake? Did you think your opinion didn't count? Were you afraid of asking a dumb question? Were you fearful that you would make a fool of yourself? Did you believe you were the only one at the meeting who didn't get it? So did you sit quietly? Did someone else say what you were thinking?
Now use the rest of your senses to *be there now.*

And now, how did you feel emotionally and psychologically about not speaking up? Did you get mad at yourself? Did you feel lesser than? Did you get sad? Did you feel like a wimp? Did you rationalize that what you wanted to say wasn't that important anyway? Did you try to convince yourself it was no big deal? Are you angry or frustrated yet? We are now going to build up your understanding of why you are holding back. Your answers:

Okay, let's move on to an earlier example.
Maybe it was three years ago at a holiday party. Who was there? Were you with friends and/or family? What were you wearing? Whose house was it? Was the house decorated in any special way? Were there children present? How many people were there? Was it daylight or evening? Were most of the people gathered in the family room or kitchen?

Again, be as specific as you can.

What was the topic of conversation? Were a few people doing most of the talking, or were people sharing the spotlight equally? Was it a lively discussion or kind of flat? Were you interested in the subject? Now use your other senses to fill in the gaps to create the best memory you can. Was there music playing? Was there food cooking? Was the dip tasty? Was it tangy, sweet, or bland? Was the furniture comfortable? The more detail the better. Okay, so . . . what did you want to say? Why didn't you? Were you afraid of making a mistake? Did you think your opinion didn't count? Were you afraid of asking a dumb question? Were you fearful that you would make a fool of yourself? Did you believe you were the only one at the party who didn't get it? So did you sit quietly? Did someone else say what you were thinking?

Now use the rest of your senses to *be there now.*

And now, how did you feel emotionally and psychologically about not speaking up? Did you get mad at yourself? Did you feel lesser than? Did you get sad? Did you feel like a wimp? Did you rationalize that what you wanted to say wasn't that important anyway? Did you try to convince yourself it was no big deal? Are you starting to see the pattern yet? Has it been going on a long time? Your answers:

Let's move on to an example from ten or fifteen years ago. You were quite a bit younger then. You could have been at a restaurant in the evening with friends or couples. What was the style of the restaurant? Greek, Italian, Indian, Asian, or all-American? How were the waiters dressed? What were you wearing? What were the decorations on the walls and ceilings? Was it crowded or slow that night? Was the place fancy or simply decorated? Was it a large room or intimate?

Now bring in your other senses. What smells were there? Was it noisy or kind of quiet? Was the food delicious or was it just okay? What was the texture of the napkins— paper or cloth? What did you want to say? Why didn't you? Were you afraid of making a mistake? Did you think your opinion didn't count? Were you afraid of asking a dumb question? Were you fearful that you would make a fool of yourself? Did you believe you were the only one at the table who didn't get it? So did you sit quietly? Did someone else say what you were thinking?

Now use the rest of your senses to *be there now.*

And now, how did you feel emotionally and psychologically about not speaking up? Did you get mad at yourself? Did you feel lesser than? Did you get sad? Did you feel like a wimp? Did you rationalize that what you wanted to say wasn't that important anyway? Did you try to convince yourself it was no big deal? Your answers:

Okay, let's move on to a very early example.
You were in first grade. You were in class. What was on the walls? What kind of desks was in the room? Was it a big room or small? About how many other students were in the classroom? Was the room full of visual aids? Was there writing on the chalkboard? What did the teacher's desk look like? What did the teacher look like? How was the teacher dressed?

Let's add your other senses. Were the chairs you sat on comfortable? Did you hear the noise through the open windows of other students playing at recess? Did you still smell the chocolate cake on your fingers left over from lunch? Do you remember how sweet it tasted?

The teacher had just asked a question:
What are the three primary colors? Okay, so what did you want to say? You thought you knew the answer—red, yellow, and blue. But you weren't sure, 100 percent sure.

You can picture yourself squirming in your chair and wanting to stand up and shout the answer. The other kids would think you were so smart. Why didn't you? Were you afraid of making a mistake? If you were wrong, they would think you were stupid and would laugh at you until you were embarrassed. Did you think your opinion didn't count?
Were you afraid of asking a dumb question? Were you fearful that you would make a fool of yourself? Did you believe you were the only one in the classroom who didn't get it? So did you sit quietly?

Did someone else say what you were thinking? Just then, while you're still squirming in your chair hesitating, Mary stands up and gives the answer: *red, yellow, and blue.* The teacher tells Mary she is correct, and most of the students look at her with admiration.

Now use the rest of your senses to *be there now.*

And now, how did you feel emotionally and psychologically about not speaking up? Did you get mad at yourself? Did you feel lesser than? Did you get sad? Did you feel like a wimp? Did you rationalize that what you wanted to say wasn't that important anyway? Did you try to convince yourself it was no big deal? Did you get mad at yourself for not taking a chance on being *wrong* or *right*? Your answers:

Whether you knew it or not, you had just begun a pattern that you would end up developing over the coming years of your life.

Is it no wonder you don't speak up *now*?

Without us even realizing it, we develop lifelong learning patterns. These patterns affect our adult lives in so many ways.

As I said earlier in the chapter, the goal of this changercise is for you to uncover some of those patterns that seem to rule your life now.

Once you recognize the power and control these fears have over you, you are then able to take constructive steps to remove those fears.

Truly invest yourself emotionally and psychologically in this changercise, and the rewards will be worth the work.

Tina O.

I'm a CEO of one of the biggest clothing chains in the world. So by now, I thought that I should be able to accomplish whatever I needed to. But the truth is, when it came to my weight, I still struggled . . .

Three months ago, I went down to my basement, closed the door, and sat in a chair. I put in my earplugs and closed my eyes. I took five deep breaths in through my nose and out through my mouth and started to relax a bit.

I have to tell you, I was really nervous. I wasn't sure why at the time. About two weeks later I figured it out. Anyway, I decided to take it slow and easy. I would recommend that to anyone who is nervous or scared. I decided I would focus on my goal *to change*—to lose weight.

I traveled back in time just a short while at first. I thought about how last week I was mad at myself. I went to put on a pair of my favorite jeans and couldn't get them to button. Now you probably think at this point that this was when I got mad at myself, but it wasn't.

Two days later, I was at the mall looking at jeans. I tried on a pair that was a size larger than the jeans that didn't fit. They fit perfectly. I walked up to the counter to pay for them. There was a customer in front of me bragging to the clerk at the register.

I couldn't help overhearing what the customer was saying. "I am rewarding myself today. Usually every fall I buy myself a pair of jeans. But I have been so good this summer that I lost enough weight to go down a size. I am so proud of myself I am buying two."

I was buying a size larger and this customer was celebrating a size smaller.

That was it. Enough was enough.

I could not bring myself to the point of buying those jeans. I put the jeans back and walked out of the store. I was mad at myself. Again!

I knew doing this changercise would be tough on me. But I felt like it was now or never.

So I traveled back a little further in time. I thought back to two years ago when almost this same thing happened, but I was two sizes smaller then. I had decided that this was as big as I was ever going to get. Again, I was mad at myself. No more chocolate cake at bedtime, or ice cream. I was going to eat healthier. I was excited I was not going to gain any more weight.

Then my grandmother died. The feeling of that loss made me depressed. I used that as the reason not to follow through with my healthy eating goal. I started gaining. And here I am today, two sizes bigger.

Okay, it really was now or never!

I decided to travel back even further, and I found a time when I was truly excited about losing weight. It was six years ago. I was looking through my old photo albums of when I was thin. I decided at the time I liked the way I looked then and made a decision to lose fifteen pounds. I remember how I felt at the time.

I made the decision. I was pumped.

I took that photo out of the album, and I put it on my bathroom mirror. Every morning and at bedtime, I would look at the mirror and the photo and card I had put next to it that said, *If it is to be it's up to me!* I really, really, wanted to look like that picture again.

Well, I am here to tell you that after three weeks I saw it beginning to work. In fact, my best friend said on the twenty-second day that there was something different about me. And it wasn't just the weight loss. There was something more.

It was a different me. My friend asked me what was going on. So I explained about my new mirror discipline.

Within six months, I was seventeen pounds lighter. Eventually, I took that picture and card off my mirror and put the picture back in the photo album. About once a month, usually on the first, I would take out that album and look at that picture. And I continued to stay that weight for three years. *I was so proud of myself.*

It was right around then that I had a falling out with my best friend and we went our separate ways. The loss caused me to get depressed. Within a year I had gained back the seventeen pounds and more.

After doing this changercise, I realized the patterns I was repeating for years. I would lose the weight. I would keep it off until I had a loss. I would get depressed and gain it back and more.

So now I know I can do it if I don't use the feeling of loss as an excuse to get depressed. I have to find a way to deal with the loss and/or depression. I now know I would use eating as a way to cope.

I began doing changercise (Silence Is Golden) once I realized what I was doing to myself. It's been helping me cope better with the feelings of loss I often feel.

I also realized, as I had once before, that if it's going to be, it's up to *me*!

So I dug out that picture and it's back on my mirror with the saying next to it.

And I am so excited; after three months I am back toward losing the extra thirty pounds I don't need or want, seven down and twenty-three to go. And this time I'm keeping an eye out for my fear of loss.

Let's look at a couple of things Tina O. learned about change.

The first thing she learned was that she needed to admit to herself that she wasn't perfect. Even as a top CEO in her industry, she was human. Losing the weight she had added on was a possibility because she had done it before.

She also learned that the changercise itself helped her to change the results by looking at the triggers that would cause her to gain the weight back again.

Pattern repetition is a very common cause of the fear of change. Learning to recognize the patterns of the past is the first step in changing them. You can't change what you don't know.

She also learned that the different changercises can work synergistically.

I found that to be true with many of my clients. They would pick more than one to do in the same week.

I also want to tell you about a bracelet I ask my clients to wear, if they want, that has printed on it the following words:

*Change the way you think and
think the way to change.*

They tell me that at various times of the week they read it and it helps them refocus in the direction they really want to go.

Go to www.changercise.com for other readers' examples and to give us your variation ideas.

Clients' comments about this changercise:

- "Recognizing that I am a visual type and seeing my internal movies of past losses in business as repeating the same scenarios for failure was an eye opener."

- "Bringing my past into the present made me miserable. Yet I kept doing it. I now realize my destiny is in my own hands."

- "Having used this changercise, I now recognize that my fear of change from when I was ten is still haunting me. I'm using the changercise Leaving the Ouch Zone to work on it, even as I send you this note."

It's time to figure out what you learned and how you can apply it to your daily/weekly/monthly work and personal life and share with other readers if you choose.

Either by using paper or your favorite electronic device, journaling these answers will help you reach your original three-sentence goal you jotted down at the very beginning of this process, in the introduction. Write out the answer to each question with thoughtful consideration.

1. How far back did you travel in time to find the pattern you keep repeating (five, ten, fifteen, twenty years)? Why are you repeating it?

2. What patterns of negative behavior did you discover in your time travels?

3. What triggers did you uncover that you still react to today?

4. How would you use this changercise to take action on a specific situation you need to change?

Share your changercise with a friend. Each of you can do the changercise and you can communicate with each other about the questions and your answers. You can communicate by text, e-mail, or the old-fashioned way, by phone. I guarantee this will speed up your ability to apply this in your daily life and help you reach your three-sentence goal that much faster.

And then make sure you share it with us at www. changercise.com and keep us in your loop.

This is all about
your choice to change.

Chapter 3
Leaving the Ouch Zone

I believe this changercise might be the hardest of all of them to do. Yet when you do this successfully, the sky's the limit for both your professional and personal growth.

What is *Leaving the Ouch Zone*?

First, I need to define what the *ouch zone* is before I can explain how to leave it.

The ouch zone is not a physical place at all. It is a place you visit—and most likely revisit—often in your mind. It is a place of pain, anger, frustration, hatred, disgust, fear, tension, regret, unforgiveness (this may not be a real word, but I sure think it is sometimes), tension, stress, loss, hopelessness, guilt, dissatisfaction, unfinished business, disappointment, sorrow, hurt, sadness, being overwhelmed, insecurity, embarrassment, depression, and yes, maybe even being minimally suicidal.

The ouch zone is, as it might seem to you, a place of pain. Leaving the ouch zone is one of the hardest changercises to do. It will help if you remind yourself of one of my favorite quotes: "Change is the essence of life. Be willing to surrender who you are for who you will become."

I created this quote years ago, but as I write *Changercise,* it continues to help me steer clearly through my *own* life.

For you to think that it is not normal—or yes, even healthy—to feel any of the previous emotions listed on the previous page, is to not be willing to admit that you are human.

For some, the ouch zone is a dark, shadowy past. For others, it is an incident you had no control over.

For others, it might be one of the following:

- loss of a family member

- divorce

- separation

- loss of a friend

- loss of a pet

- Dear John text

- loss of a house

- loss of a job/business

- injured body part

- an argument with a friend

- an argument with a loved one

- loss of a dream

- loss of independence

- perceived loss of choice

- words wished unsaid by you or others

- a host of other pains

Go to www.changercise.com to give us your ouch zone ideas.

Now you know what the ouch zone is.

You know that loss and pain require grieving and healing time. In no way am I suggesting that you don't go through those periods. I am talking about when it becomes excessive or even obsessive.

I want you to take some quality time now and write down at least three ouch zones that you often revisit throughout your week. Be as specific as you can.

Later, when you do this changercise, you will focus on using your five senses to really be there in that experience, just like you did in the time traveler changercise.

Sometimes you will actually find comfort in your ouch zone. Yes, I admit that there are times when I do as well. It is a place of familiarity and, in a strange way, comfortability. You know of times in your life when you were (or you might be right now) in a comparison match. And you are going for the title of most pain, hurt, sadness . . . you fill in the blank.

It usually starts out rather mundane and simple. One person starts to talk about their previous partner, or maybe a car accident they were in, or a recent or past surgery they had. Before you know it, the conversation is escalating to where the pain factor has reached such a piercing level that you are doing a one-upmanship about thinking about suicide.

If you think I'm being overly dramatic, just go to a company lunch room, where there are some people who have such a strong need for attention that they spill their guts for a bit of recognition.

Have you seen any local newscasts lately? They are filled with family members or neighbors talking about the latest tragedy in their lives. For that matter, have you seen many of the talk shows that now center on the misfortune of one family or relationship against another? For some, it is a public showing of their ouch zone that brings them some comfort. For others, it is a more private affair.

You can commiserate with coworkers, friends and loved ones, or even by yourself. You can get attention and even love for being in the ouch zone. You can get pity, sympathy, and empathy as well. So getting that attention is better sometimes—maybe most of the time—than no attention at all.

The problem becomes—due to this attention, and against your better judgment—you don't want to leave. And although you know emotionally, logically, and psychologically that it would be best to do so, you hang on to the past for comfort of some kind. For many, it is an addiction.

Why do Leaving the Ouch Zone?

The OZ is a very unhappy place. So this question, for this changercise, seems rather silly at first glance.

Unlike the previous changercises that seem to be a bit more optional, you would think that everyone would want to leave his or her OZ. And although it is probably true that everyone would *want* to leave, most either don't know how and/or don't want to do the work to leave.

Here is the section I gave as a preview in both the introduction and chapter 1.

Speaking with many of my clients through the years, I have seen the following three facts emerge related to this particular changercise:

1. No matter how negative the results of being in your ouch zone (OZ) might be, you still find positive pieces in your own personal OZs—pieces that fill a need of some kind.

2. You are a creature of habit, and it is often easier to just keep doing what you've always done, whether that is driving the same route to work or holding on to pain and suffering with it.

3. For my clients who are willing to suspend disbelief, to do the hard work of change, this changercise catapults you months and sometimes years ahead of where you would be without it. Faith is a powerful catalyst for change.

This changercise is for you when you have decided it's time to move on! Only you will decide the appropriate time. But all too often you know you *should but can't.* This changercise is designed to help those of you who *can't.*

How do you leave the ouch zone?

Before I tell you how to do this I must give you a warning . . .

I will tell you now that this will take strength, guts, fierceness, determination, and—most of all—focus of purpose.

I want to remind you that this will not be easy. I have fought this fight many times over in my life. It is not for the faint of heart or the lightweight.

But this is a fight that must be pursued by the heavyweight in you if you are to regain and become who you really are meant to be.

So here is your dilemma. Do you hold on to the pain in whatever form it is in and the comfort it brings you? Or do you:

Change the way you think and think the way to change?

Remember, your clock is ticking. You are not getting any younger. You choose.

Of course, as with any changercise, it is your choice to do it or not to do it.

This changercise will take a giant leap of belief and faith.

Again, the definition of *belief* in dictionary.com is *confidence in the truth or existence of something not immediately susceptible to rigorous proof.*

So for this changercise to work well, *you* are going to create the confidence in the truth or existence of something not immediately susceptible to rigorous proof. For many, the words *belief* and *faith* are interchangeable. For purposes of simplifying this process, I will use them that way.

So that means that you must *suspend disbelief,* even if you think it is childish, false, or ignorant.

Remember I said *giant* leap of faith and *belief.*

There are—and I'm sure in the future there will be many— techniques to break out, break away, or break through to a new beginning. And although, ultimately, this changercise will have the same results as many others, *it is the approach that is unique.*

In some ways, this changercise works just the opposite way of what you may have expected. Instead of breaking away, breaking through, or breaking out, you are going to *dive* right in.

How do you leave the ouch zone?

Find a quiet and safe place where you can be alone and uninterrupted for at least thirty to sixty minutes—and where you can be loud *if necessary.*

If you want, you can ask someone to guide you through this changercise, reading this like a script you can follow step by step. Or you can do it by yourself. Whether you have someone guide you or you do it yourself, your results may be some of the most intense feelings you've had for quite a while.

You may experience any number of these reactions: yelling, pounding, clenched fists of rage, deep sadness that will bring you to tears, loud laughter, coughing, shaking, or possibly suicidal feelings and hopelessness.

Remember, I said this changercise is for the heavyweight fighter in you

Do not do this changercise just because it's in this book. You can skip it if you feel you aren't ready for it.

Make sure you're ready. And I repeat, *do this changercise by choice.*

Okay. Have I given you enough warnings? I certainly think I have. This is your last chance to skip to chapter 4.

Sit back. Take a deep breath, in through your nose and out through your mouth. (From here on out, when I say take a deep breath that is how I want you to do it.) If closing your eyes helps, you can do so. Of course to do that you will need to memorize this process (unless you want to peek out from your squinting eyes to read the next step, which some folks actually choose to do).

I want you to begin to be aware of all five of your senses as you sit where you are. Listen to the noises around you, the feeling of your back, your butt, your arms and legs, your breathing, the taste in your mouth, what you see around you if your eyes are open, or what you see in the darkness of your eyelids if they are closed, the scents and smells around you, and the way all your senses affect your awareness of the moment.

You are now going to create a baseline for your healthy zone (HZ). This will require you to amplify your senses.

For a better understanding of how to amplify your senses, I will use two examples: first my auditory sense and then my visual sense. Both will be while I am sitting at my kitchen table.

First, the auditory sense.

In a typical moment there are lots of sounds all around me. At 0 amplification I am typically only hearing the thoughts in my head. Now I want to amplify the sounds by 1. I hear the hum of the fan from my air conditioner. I hear the ticking of a clock. Now I amplify that sense by 2. I hear the ice machine and the hum of my computer fan. And now I amplify by 3. At this intense level of sound, I hear all the items mentioned, plus I hear the slight creak as I move ever so slightly in my chair. I hear what sounds like a jet engine in my ears, and a motorcycle as it drives by outside my kitchen window.

Now for the visual sense.

In a typical moment there are lots of images all around me. At 0 amplification I am typically only viewing the images that are directly in front of me on my kitchen table. Now I want to amplify my viewing by 1. I see the paintings on the walls, the ceiling fixtures, and the faint white streak on my kitchen floor. Now I amplify my sense by 2. The painting of the barn, near the hutch in the kitchen, is more yellow than it usually is. I see the walls and ceiling fixtures in the family room across from my kitchen. The colors are more alive. What used to look like a dull brown carpet is now more vivid like the color of hot chocolate. The boat painting in the family room above the couch has a lot more red in it. And now I amplify by 3. At this intense level of viewing, I see all the items mentioned, plus I see the scratches on the kitchen table, the gray smudged thumbprint by the light switch, the bright blue waves and whitecaps on the boat painting in the family room, and I even catch a glimpse of the motorcycle as it drives by outside my kitchen window.

With each amplification, I become even more aware of the depth of my sensations. I notice the difference between 0 and 1, 1 and 2, 2 and 3. I notice how at each level I become more aware of my environment and my surroundings. The more I let my senses run wild with abandonment like a kid in a candy store, the better my ultimate results will be.

By the time I get to 3, my sensations are cascading over me as a new reality emerges of my senses and my surroundings.

Now, I want you to pick at least one of your five senses and do the amplify part of this changercise, using the previous examples as a guide—and then journal your impressions.

This is what is real; this is what is now. Remember these sensations. This is where you will return (to your HZ) with a new exuberance for life and living once you've experienced Leaving the Ouch Zone (OZ).

Let's start by looking at *your* OZ. You may want to pick one that is fairly harmless, or you can use your most prominent OZ. It's your choice. And keep in mind that you may want to do this changercise for more than one OZ. Of course my clients and I highly recommend doing them separately, one at a time, with either hours or day(s) in between. Trust me; one at a time is plenty if done correctly.

Journal a description of the OZ with which you are going to start.

I'm going to guide you through this OZ changercise by giving you a personal example of an OZ of mine that I carried around with me for years.

I'll put my answers to this changercise in *italics*.

Begin by starting to think about your OZ. Think about all the feelings you associate with your OZ. Think about the first moment it became a thought, a reality for you. It could have been last month or last year, five or twenty years ago. It makes no difference. *It was six or seven years after I got married.* Think about it as though it just happened five minutes ago.

Where were you when it began? *I was in the kitchen of my new home.* What were you thinking the moment before it happened? *I was happy that my father had come to visit.* Who was with you? *My wife, my father and mother-in-law, and my father.* What were you talking about? *Just chit-chatting about our new home.*

What scents and smells were there? *I remember my wife and I were baking a pumpkin pie. It's one of my favorites.* What were you doing with your hands, your feet, and your body? *I was very physically relaxed at that moment.* What was the taste in your mouth? *I was chewing some blueberry gum.*

What did you see straight in front of you, to your left, and to your right? What was directly behind you? *I was starting to walk from the kitchen toward the family room where my father and my father-in-law were talking. That's when it happened. I froze in my tracks before I reached the family room. I overheard my father say to my father-in-law, "Ya know, I never really thought he would amount to somethin'." That felt like he had put a dagger in my heart. I guess I never realized how poorly he thought about my prospects as a man and a provider for a family someday. For many years to come that would be one of my biggest ouch zones.*

Okay, now it's your turn.

Begin by starting to think about your OZ. Think about all the feelings you associate with your OZ. Think about the first moment it became a thought, a reality for you. It could have been last month or last year, five or twenty years ago. It makes no difference.

Think about it as though it just happened five minutes ago.

Where were you when it began? What were you thinking the moment before it happened? Who was with you? What were you talking about?

What scents and smells were there? What were you doing with your hands, your feet, and your body? What was the taste in your mouth?

What did you see straight in front of you, to your left, and to your right? What was directly behind you?

Journal your answers.

Go back to that situation that just happened "five minutes ago." Now, as you use your five senses, start by amplifying them by 1, then 2, and finally by 3. Remember to breathe throughout this changercise.

Feelings and emotions will begin to emerge and start to amplify. You may want to pound something in anger, or scream out in disgust or disappointment. You may start to feel tension and tightening in your neck or back muscles.

You may want to yell at someone using very harsh words. You may want to cry a little or sob uncontrollably. You may want to just crawl up in a ball in your chair like a baby. You may talk to yourself out loud or inwardly. You may want to sit quietly and feel sorry for yourself.

You may want to stop the changercise right then and there. You may want to start telling your side of the story. No matter what you think or feel or want to do (except hurt someone or break something you'll regret later), it is okay.

There are lots of different ways to respond. This is to say that you have permission to delve deep into those negative feelings. Let yourself truly feel the anger, the pain, the sadness, the fear, or whatever else is welling up inside you. The more you let your imagination unfold freely, the more this will help you later.

Remember to breathe throughout this changercise.

Now I want you to imagine—while feeling all these feelings and emotions at level 3—that it is six months from now and you are still feeling them. This will surely intensify any number of new feelings as well. Take a moment and observe your feelings, your thoughts, and your sensations.

Now move to one year from now. Notice if things have changed—or are they the same? Have they intensified? Or are you becoming numb?

Now go five years into the future and still feel these emotions, feelings, and thoughts. This is your OZ. You've created it. Stay there for a few more moments. How ya doin'? You're probably not feeling too well. Do you have a sore back or knees, headache or tension in your hands? Do you feel like your stomach is in knots, or that you might vomit on the spot? All these responses are necessary and to be expected. This is a painful experience. Hold it another moment . . .

Remember to breathe.

Now I want you to create an image that represents your OZ. It could be a shoe, a house, a baseball field, a car, a hospital, a backpack, an office building, an elevator, or a briefcase. Come up with some kind of visual representation of your OZ. Remember it well.

By the way, do you want to go for ten years into the future? If you want, you could even *take your OZ to your grave.*

Remember, it's your choice; it is your OZ and no one else's. Is it serving you well? Is it getting you closer to what you need and want? Are you finding this OZ of yours a good place to be?

Journal your thoughts and feelings.

Had enough? Are you ready to leave?

Wait!

Look at the function it is serving. Is it getting you the attention you so desperately need? Might there be another way to do that? Is it filling a need to feel sorry for yourself or someone else? Is it working as a good excuse so you don't have to move on? Does it help you procrastinate?

Journal your thoughts and feelings.

Need more pain? No? You say you're ready to experience Leaving the Ouch Zone.

Okay, let's leave your OZ. Take all those emotions and thoughts and feelings and *in your imagination* stuff them in a shoe, house, baseball field, car, backpack, office building, elevator, briefcase, or whatever you chose for your representation. Once you've done that, I want you to figure out a real cool way to get rid of the representation and all its contents (only in your mind of course).

Here are a few examples of how my clients have done this:

1. Shoe—throw it off a cliff; have a tiger rip it to shreds by putting a piece of meat in it.
2. Baseball field—spread it all over the grass and have a lawnmower grind it up.
3. House—have it disappear in a sinkhole.
4. Backpack—have it stolen by an unsuspecting robber.
5. Briefcase—attach helium balloons to it and have it float away.

Now come up with your own creative idea for its destruction. Other clients have visualized using a bomb, fire, lightning bolt, burning acid, or some other very violent way of creating destruction. Be as creative as you choose. It is your OZ and you have every right to destroy it however you like.

Journal it here.

This part of the changercise always seems to be "fun" to share with friends.

Move one mile away and use a telescope to see that tiny OZ in the distance. Destroy it! Now watch its destruction. How ya feeling now? Now leave the five years into the future behind you (I hope you didn't choose ten years or the grave) and go to one year into the future.

Maybe by now you've said to yourself, *There is no way that I want to still be in my OZ five years from now.* Great . . . good work. We are making progress.

Now it is one year from now. Destroy it again, but this time with more fervor and joy as you see it disappear. This time I want you to get in your imaginary car and drive five miles away. Now get out your super-powered telescope and view that tiny thing, your OZ. Feeling better yet? So now you know for sure there is no way you are willing to accept this OZ in your life for even a year from now. Terrific.

Ready for six months? Now for some of you, this time frame will actually be harder to do than a one-month-from-now time frame. (I'll explain why later.)

This time I want you to not just put all your emotions, thoughts, and feelings in this representation you are going to destroy; I want you to include your feelings and thoughts that you didn't even know you had. Do you know which ones I'm talking about? I'm referring to that little guilt that is hiding under the table from you, the tiny bit of sadness and feel-sorry-for-myself that doesn't want to come out and play—the last piece of anger that is afraid to show its face. All of these and the rest that are hiding need to be destroyed this time.

Now get in your helicopter and view that tiny past OZ of yours from the air. But before it's destroyed, take the time to fly around a bit and notice all that is good with your world. See if you can spot happy and content people. You'll find them if you look for them. So the destruction takes place and it looks so tiny from so high up that you can barely notice it. It has become a nonissue for you. It's as if that was the past, not the future.

It is time to live your life through the eyes of today. Too often you live your life through yesterday's eyes. You are what you believe. Your belief system is based on your past experiences. These experiences are being constantly relived in your present. So you anticipate your future being like your past. It's time to live through the eyes of today.

And that is exactly what it truly was, your *OZ Past.* For some, this will end this part of the changercise. You will begin to concentrate on your five senses and the awareness you had at the beginning of this changercise. Listen to the noises around you, the feelings of your back, your butt, your arms and legs, your breathing, the taste in your mouth, what you see around you if your eyes are open, or what you see in the darkness of your eyelids if they are closed, the scents and smells around you, and the way this affects your awareness of the moment.

Now, I want you to amplify all of this by 1, then 2, then 3. And very quickly you will have trouble even knowing what your OZ was that you were so upset about. *At that point it will be cascading over you as a new reality that this is what is real; this is what is now.* And for you, your changercise is done.

For those who still feel like there is still a piece of your OZ left, you can do this changercise once a week for a month until that thirty days into the future is real and you have left your OZ for good.

Tommy H.

I am a sales team leader in a division at a Fortune 500 company now. I knew that if I wanted to be a better leader and move up in my company I would need to get rid of "certain thoughts and emotions" I was holding on to from a bad experience at my previous job. I began to think about my OZ. My OZ began five months ago. I can remember it as though it happened yesterday. On a conference call, we were told that the company wanted to save money and so had decided that our sales division was no longer profitable and was being dissolved in thirty days. You could have heard the proverbial pin drop, it was so quiet.

I remember thinking, *You didn't even give us a fighting chance to prove our value, you just kicked us to the curb like an unwanted pair of sneakers that had run the race and was no longer relevant.* I had been a loyal company man for fifteen years, and this is how they treat me. I was angry and resentful. All the salespeople kept reliving the drama over and over again as we sat in the break room. It went on for four weeks until we were all let go. It was so depressing hearing everyone keep repeating the same thing.

So here I was, five months later, and I knew it was time for me to change. So I started by creating a baseline for my healthy zone (HZ).

Sitting on a warm summer's day on my little deck off my kitchen, I could hear the drone of a lawnmower coming from my neighbor's yard. I began to amplify to 1. As I listened closer, I could hear the chirps of the many birds from the surrounding yards. All at once the mower stopped. The birds seemed to get louder. I then realized I was getting bitten by mosquitoes. I quickly went inside, grabbed my torch lighter, came back out and lit my mini tiki torches that keep the mosquitoes at bay.

To amplify my feeling sense to 1, I let myself really feel the itching that was now coming from the bites. As I began to amplify my sense of smell, just then a bit of a breeze picked up, and I could smell the flame from the torches. I saw the wind playing with the leaves in the trees. Just then the mower started again.

This is when I decided to amplify my senses to 2. I closed my eyes and heard a plane passing by. I could feel the softness of the cushion I was sitting on against my butt and back. I could still taste the residue of the iced tea I had an hour ago. As I breathed, I could feel my chest moving up and down. The smell of the tiki torches seemed to get stronger. I heard an acorn fall from a tree branch.

I had a new friend by now. It was a fly that continued to circle around me. Then it landed on my arm and created just enough of a tickle to feel it. At that moment I began to remind myself of the beauty that was surrounding me. I let myself focus and delve deep into the joy of the beauty of the day.

Now with real anticipation, I chose to go to level 3. Just then the lawnmower started up again. I could feel a very small headache forming from the intensity of my focus and concentration, and that was okay. I could feel the hair on my head move from the gentle breezes that were coming and going. I could see one lonely cloud as it slowly passed overhead in a beautiful, powder blue sky. It reminded me of the crest of an ocean wave.

The black smoke residue and scent from the tiki torches seemed to grow even stronger. I felt the little bit of saliva between my tongue and lips. My five senses were truly heightened, and I had done it by my choices of what to focus on. I was in my HZ. It was just after that thought that I started to get excited about leaving my OZ.

So I began the OZ portion of this changercise. I thought about my OZ as though it just happened five minutes ago.

When it began, I was sitting in my office. The thoughts I was having the moment just before it happened were about wondering why we were having this "emergency" conference call. It seemed a bit strange. I remember a faint smell that was always present from the plant in the corner. I could hear the humming of my computer. My office door was closed. I could still taste the licorice candy I had just finished. I was squeezing a pen as I heard the news.

Up until that point it seemed like leaving my OZ was a nice theory. I began to realize that I had lost that feeling of relaxation combined with joy and exhilaration. So I knew I was ready to continue the changercise that would start me on my journey of leaving the OZ. I was nervous and anxious.

So now I amplify it by 1.

I chose to use my imagination as if I was in a boat on a lake when I heard the news.

I'm confused. I am adrift in a boat in the middle of a lake with no motor and no paddles. I am sad. A whole piece of my life is disappearing. What will I do now? That is who I was for fifteen years. I want to run away and come back to find out none of it was true. But it was.

I start to make fists and feel the back of my legs tighten up. I start to get sleepy and want to take a nap. Could someone please throw me a life preserver? It's hopeless.

I'm ready to amplify to 2, and so I do so immediately.

Now I'm in the boat and there are large waves in the lake that are throwing the boat and me from side to side. There are man-eating fish just within reach that are waiting for a hand or foot to accidentally slip out of the boat, for they haven't had their lunch yet. I can see people on the shoreline and I am yelling to them to call the patrol boats to come and rescue me, but they can't hear my shouting over the roar of the waves. I'm really getting very angry.

I have lost all my patience and I am fed up with my inability to control the direction of the boat. And then I finally notice that there are many more boats in the water just like me. And they are all screaming and shouting to the people on the shoreline but they are not being heard either.

My eyes feel like they are burning, and my breathing is getting heavier. I am getting more scared and I don't know what to do next.

So I amplify to level 3. And that is when the guilt begins to raise its ugly face. It is a shark snapping at me as it makes passes at my boat every five minutes and I am terrified. What did I do to deserve this? Why is this happening to me?

I was always willing to pull my weight with the company. Even if there were times I didn't want to do it their way, I would bite the bullet and do so. I ask myself every five minutes, *What could I have done differently to avoid this?* Why didn't I see it coming? What a fool I was not to recognize the signs.

And that is when I notice the hole at the front of the boat and the water starting to seep in. I am terrified. I take a rag and plug the hole. The water stops coming in for the moment. And another shark passes by.

There's four inches of water in the boat and I know it's just a matter of time before one of the sharks does more than just swim by. My chest is tight and my back aches. And my jaw is clenched.

I am scared and sad.

This is my OZ. As I picture myself six months from now feeling this way, I get angry. And though I know it is imaginary, this is how I feel. And I also feel sad for myself that I have wasted my time letting this get to me. It makes me want to yell and scream . . . enough is enough. So I scream as loud as I can and it hurts so much.

Now I am picturing one year forward still living in my OZ. I am really getting angrier . . . how dare that company I worked for that is no longer paying me still have control over my life at this point? I am now feeling determined that this *giving control up to my emotions* has to end.

So then I take it out five years and I am disgusted with myself. I am so disappointed that I gave up and let my negative emotions win out.

I really let myself feel the anguish and heartache of living in my OZ five years from now. It was so depressing. It meant I had let go of so many of my dreams and goals.

I was going to let the past rob me of a happier future life.

I started to cry, and then I started sobbing. I clenched my fists on my desk and pounded it and said, "This must stop and I must stop it! I am ready and willing to do whatever it takes. I am leaving the ouch zone now, before it's too late."

I can still make sure this future doesn't become my reality.

So, in my imagination, three different times, I took all those emotions of pain and anger and frustration and disappointment and more, and I took all the tools of my old job and I stuffed them all into a briefcase. Then I walked with it to the shoreline of the lake, I put it in a boat, and pushed it out toward the middle of the lake.

The first time, five years into the future, I got on my bike and road a mile away. The second time, one year into the future, I got in a car and road five miles away. By then I had realized one year was too long. So six months into the future, I got in my helicopter and flew far away. The first two times, I would take out my telescope, once I was far enough away, and set it up on the tripod.

When I found the briefcase in the scope, I pushed the button on my handheld detonator, watched it blow a hole in the boat, and watched the briefcase as it sank to the bottom of the lake, along with my OZ.

By the third time, I was in the air on my helicopter when, off in the distance, I heard a faint explosion. The automatic timer had gone off. I looked at my watch and knew that the briefcase would be at the bottom of the lake, its final resting place, in about forty-five seconds.

The relief I felt around me was amazing. I physically felt lighter. I was now feeling even better knowing those dreadful feelings wouldn't be with me even six months from now, let alone ten years. For the first time I didn't even need to see it sink. It was no longer part of my life. It was the past. I knew that it was no longer important to me and had no control over my emotions or me. I knew what leaving the OZ was all about.

I knew for me, even six months was no longer an option for any of my other OZs that I was living in. So for the next nine weeks in a row, I visited a different OZ each time. And as I got more familiar and creative with the changercise, I found that one year was the farthest I needed to go to feel the depth of pain and need to change.

If I could say one thing, it would be that this changercise has been a lifesaver for me. And, although it takes a lot of hard work and emotional diving, the results are ten times worth it. I actually now look forward to my imaginary helicopter rides, when I need them. They are now few and far between.

Also, I often read the "change the way you think" bracelet I got from you. There are times when just reading it at a particular moment in the day helps me refocus my direction.

Now, when I am around people and their OZ, I can recognize it. I know how to stay in my own thoughts and emotions. And as a manager that had a team of seventy-five people, it was essential for me to have those skills to have been able to lead them successfully. I say this in the past tense, because I received that promotion and am now the head of my division.

Let's look at a couple of things Tommy H. learned about change.

He realized that if he wanted to be a better leader and move up in his company, he would need to get rid of certain thoughts and emotions he was holding on to from a bad experience at his previous job.

He learned how to create a baseline for his healthy zone (HZ) and let himself focus and delve deep into the joy of the beauty of the day.

He realized that even six months was no longer an option for holding on to any of his other OZs that he was living in.

And he learned how to stay in his own thoughts and emotions by remembering he doesn't need to live in other people's dramas.

Go to www.changercise.com for other readers' examples and to give us your variation ideas.

So you do this changercise because it is ultimately good for your psyche, your attitude, your strength of mind and emotion, and for your overall sense of well-being. It lightens your load. It gives you room to breathe.

And after you have done a few, over a month's period of time, you can see clearly how to make effective decisions from a place of healthy thoughts and emotions, not from a painful history.

Clients' comments about this changercise:

- "At fifty years old, I went twenty years into the future. I realized I better face the pain of my baby son's death now instead of living in the ouch zone until I was seventy. I'm still working on it, a week at a time."

- "I have to tell you, although this changercise is supposed to be painful, I really enjoyed destroying an ouch zone I had lurking around. And thanks for the change bracelet. I read it daily."

- "Some hurt is so hard to get rid of. Using this changercise over a year's period of time, I was able to finally release it. It's been such a relief, finally!"

It's time to figure out what you learned and how you can apply it to your daily/weekly/monthly work and personal life and share with other readers if you choose.

Either by using paper or your favorite electronic device, journaling these answers will help you reach your original three-sentence goal you jotted down at the very beginning of this process, in the introduction. Write out the answer to each question with thoughtful consideration.

1. What was your ouch zone? How long ago did you create it?

2. By what destructive method did you choose to get rid of your ouch zone?

3. How long are you willing to live with your current ouch zones? Thirty days? Six months? One year, five years, or ten years? What are you waiting for?

4. How would you use this changercise to take action on a specific situation you need to change?

Share your changercise with a friend. Each of you can do the changercise and you can communicate with each other about the questions and your answers. You can communicate by text, e-mail, or the old-fashioned way, by phone. I guarantee this will speed up your ability to apply this in your daily life and help you reach your three-sentence goal that much faster.

And then make sure you share it with us at www. changercise.com and keep us in your loop.

*This is all about
your choice to change.*

Chapter 4
Who's Laughing Now?

This changercise is all about having a joyful attitude.

What is *Who's Laughing Now*?

This, by far, is the most fun and longest-lasting changercise of them all!

I continue to use this changercise when I do my early-morning daily walks. Not only does it make the time go by faster, but it makes for an enjoyable and entertaining walk.

Let's get one or two things clear from the beginning. If you are concerned about *Who's Laughing Now* at *you*, then you are focused in the wrong direction—unless of course you are in comedy and you make your living getting people to laugh at you. In that case, get as many people laughing at you as you can.

Now, back to the changercise. I am, of course, talking about laughter that bellows forth *from you*. I am therefore talking about old-fashioned, out loud belly laughing. You know the kind. You start laughing and before you know it, it's hard to stop. You laugh so hard it seems like your stomach is going to burst. You have trouble catching your breath. You are so caught up that tears roll from your eyes.

The cause of this laughter is available to you in many forms:

- newspaper comic section

- favorite radio station

- late-night TV talk show host's monologue

- favorite YouTube videos

- favorite comedy blog

- favorite LinkedIn or Facebook comedy group posts

- favorite joke book

- favorite TV show on the comedy channel

- favorite CD or DVD comedy album

- favorite comedy podcast

- community theater

- movie theater

- high school theater

- old record comedy albums

- comedy club in town

- best friends telling their favorite jokes

- favorite jokes told by you or someone else

- looking at yourself in the mirror (Hey, that's a joke! Relax, I was just kidding.)

Where do you find laughter? Journal it here.

Why do Who's Laughing Now?

Just imagine if you did a changercise that helped you think good thoughts and feel good every Saturday. Wow, what a great weekend you would have. Maybe even a great week.

Imagine how you would be perceived by other people (of course not the ones who heard you belly laughing in your space void of sound). I mean all the rest of those grumpy, disappointed, depressed, and sad people you come in contact with on a weekly basis. Some of them, even your closest relationships, might actually ask you why you are so *damn* happy.

Then you can tell them about this changercise. Who knows, maybe they'll try it out for themselves.

Okay, well, you can dream, can't you?

Anyway, at least you'll be happy until the next Saturday.

*This is all about
your choice to change.*

Here are some other people's opinions of what humor can do for you, based on a quick web search:

- Humor combats fear.
- Humor comforts.
- Humor relaxes.
- Humor reduces pain.
- Humor boosts the immune system.
- Humor reduces stress.
- Humor helps to communicate.
- Humor spreads happiness.
- Humor helps heal the body after surgery.

See the references section for more details.

What would you like to change through your own laughter?

How do you do Who's Laughing Now?

As you read at the beginning of this chapter, this is, by far, the most fun and longest lasting changercise of them all!

Here is why I say this.

You will need to establish if the time you spend doing this changercise is worth it to you. This may take some real digging.

Let me explain . . .

Here's how to do Who's Laughing Now?

In the beginning, you'll need at least ten minutes for this changercise. Find a safe place where you can be very loud.

I mean VERY LOUD!

Maybe it's the same location where you do the changercise Silence Is Golden.

(Find a place that is void of sound . . .)

Now let me digress for a moment. Prior to going to this place, you need to find the material you will listen to and/or watch.

Be very selective, as you want these ten minutes to be side-splittingly funny.

In preparation for this changercise you may need to do a voice recording of you or someone else telling those jokes. Or you may need to record from the radio, the Internet, a CD or TV. Or there may be a funny video from YouTube. Maybe you will need to record at a live theater performance or comedy club. You may need to record yourself reading a blog post, or piece of a website, or maybe reading multiple comic strips from your newspaper. Maybe the jokes or funny stories are on what we used to call a *record album* (with comedians like Bill Cosby, George Carlin, or Jack Benny).

Journal how you prepared the audio/video.

Okay. So we will assume that you have now prepared the audio and/or video for your listening and/or viewing pleasure.

Now go to that safe place *void of sound* and fill it with comedy. Sit or stand—I prefer sitting—and *immerse yourself in pure hilarity!*

I'm talking about total immersion. So from the top of your head to the bottom of your feet, you are totally immersed.

My goal for you in this changercise is for you to be laughing so hard and loud that you become hysterical (definition of hysterical from Webster's Dictionary: *impossible to hold back or control {laughter}*). Giving yourself permission to let yourself go will be a big challenge for many of you.

Remember, this is good for your mental as well as physical health.

Warning before you start . . . Please let anyone who could hear you—anyone—know what you are doing. If you don't, and they hear you, they may think you have become *hysterical*, and they might call the authorities.

Let 'er rip. I want you to *make some noise!* Now really get into it with all your senses. See the visual descriptions in your mind's eye, hear the loudness of funniness (not sure if that's a real term or not, oh well), smell the scents of humor, (get it, *scents*), taste its comical sweetness, and last but not least, feel the gut-wrenching, side-splitting spasms that are going through your body at this moment.

Your endorphins are zooming all around the room—figuratively, of course. Not only will you be laughing loudly, you will most likely have tears in your eyes from such extreme comedy, hence the expression, "I laughed so hard I cried." Or, for some who truly become *hysterical*, you may even *wet your pants*.

You'll feel invigorated, ready, and looking forward to taking on the rest of your day. Now, if for some reason that's not happening . . .

There are two reasons for this:

   1. You have not truly *let yourself go.*

or

   2. You have picked material that's *not funny enough.*

There are two solutions for this:

   1. *Let yourself go . . .*

or

2. *Find new material.*

Either way, you need to get those stomachaches that everyone else gets who does this changercise successfully.

I am going to assume from this point forward that you either fell into the successful category the first time, *or* you worked on solution 1 or 2 until you were finally successful.

Garrett B.

For me, the funniest guy in the world is Bill Cosby. Now, I like Jon Stewart, all the guys from the Blue Collar Comedy Tour (especially Jeff Foxworthy), Sinbad, Lewis Black, Ellen DeGeneres, Lily Tomlin, Margaret Cho, Whoopi Goldberg, Jerry Seinfeld, Dane Cook, Brian Regan, Jeff Dunham, Robin Williams, George Carlin, and many others.

But I think Bill is the best of them all. Now, I am sure you will disagree—and that is certainly your right—but too bad. This is my example, not yours. Just kidding, of course.

My favorite albums (yes, I said *albums*) are *Why Is There Air*; *To Russell, My Brother, Whom I Slept With*; *I Started Out as a Child*; and my absolute favorite, *Bill Cosby Is a Very Funny Fellow . . . Riiiight!* It is this album that has the single where he is Noah talking to the Lord who is telling him to build an ark because he, the Lord, is going to destroy the world . . . *Riiiight!* It is so hilarious.

Just writing this right now is putting a smile on my face. So what I did was to burn a CD that consisted of Cosby, Stewart, Cho, Regan, and Foxworthy. The first time I actually played the whole thing—which was about fifteen minutes long—it was a real breakthrough. I played it while I was sitting in our employees' parking lot after work in my car one day.

I really am glad I had the CD ready to go. That day was a really tough one. As the lead on my sales team, I had to deal with three belligerent clients in a row. Normally after a day like that, I would drive home, and while sitting in traffic, start to fume and get even more frustrated and angry.

By the time I would get home, I was a bear. And I would often then take it out on my wife by getting in a fight about something that was so silly. I would then end up sulking the rest of the evening. Sometimes I would admit what an idiot I was and apologize, and sometimes I wouldn't.

So here I am listening to the CD, and I laughed so hard I almost wet my pants. By the time those fifteen minutes had gone by, those idiot clients of mine were history.

After listening, I sat and thought how important laughter was in my life. I forgot that, being so busy with work and life. I realized I needed to incorporate more *funny time* into my life. I burned four CDs with different mixes of my favorites. At least twice a week, in the evenings, I began listening to them for fifteen minutes.

After about the third week of doing this, I started to get comments from my associates. One said, "What have you been smokin'? You seem to be much happier in the last few weeks. What are you doing different?" So I told him. The other person said, "Garrett, what's up with you? You're so relaxed and patient. It's as if you're a different person". So I told her too.

Two weeks later, she told me she made a comedy mix CD of her own and she was listening to it at home on Sunday evenings. She thanked me for the idea. She said she was *hooked*. I told her, I would rather be *hooked* on this than many other things I could be *hooked* on. She agreed.

All I can say is that if you don't do this changercise once in a while at the least, you're missing the boat. I realized that I owe it to myself to do this. And I think you do too!

Let's look at a couple of things Garrett B. learned about change.

He learned that because he was so busy with work and personal stuff, he had shut out *funny time* from his life.

He realized that by being consistent with his funny time, he was getting real results. And even his coworkers noticed it.

He found that a good dose of funny time helped put things in perspective, especially troublesome clients.

Although this seems like a very simple changercise, almost common sense, it is not. The key to this changercise is to get to the gut level of emotion of funny time.

Go to www.changercise.com for other readers' examples and to give us your *funny time* ideas.

An article in the *Harvard Health Blog*, from November 2010, says, "There's a lot of data showing that patients who are depressed after heart surgery have a higher mortality rate, and optimistic patients have significantly fewer wound infections. Deep laughter reduces the level of stress hormones: cortisol, epinephrine (adrenaline), dopamine, and growth hormone. It also increases the level of health-enhancing hormones like endorphins. Laughter increases the number of antibody-producing cells we have working for us, and enhances the effectiveness of T cells."

In 2006, researchers led by Stanley A. Tan and Lee Berk at Loma Linda University in Loma Linda, California, found that two hormones—beta-endorphins (which alleviate depression) and human growth hormone (HGH, which helps with immunity)—increased by 27 and 87 percent, respectively, when volunteers anticipated watching a humorous video. Simply anticipating laughter boosted health-protecting hormones and chemicals.

In his "American Fitness" article, Dave Traynor explains a separate study at Arkansas Tech University, in which concentrations of immunoglobulin A were increased after twenty-one fifth graders participated in a humor program. (I'm nervous to hear about the details of that fifth-grade humor program, because my kids roar whenever you throw out a bathroom term.) Laughter was once again found to increase the ability to fight viruses and foreign cells.

You can find more details in the references section.

Clients' comments about this changercise:

- "This is my favorite changercise. I had become so serious. You know, with all the negative news bombarding me every day and the stress of work. Now that I do this changercise regularly, even my wife is happier. Thanks, DW."

- "This changercise is a lifesaver, literally. After my heart attack I knew something had to change . . . and in a hurry. Now not only do I feel healthier, but also my doctor said I am healthier. Laughter is the best medicine."

- "My team—I'm a division manager—says I'm so much easier to talk to now. Of course, I give all the credit to Jerry Seinfeld, Robin Williams, and especially Whoopi Goldberg."

It's time to figure out what you learned and how you can apply it to your daily/weekly/monthly work and personal life and share with other readers if you choose.

1. Who did you choose for your best comedians list for your listening pleasure?

2. Who, what, when, where, and how did you do this changercise?

3. How has humor made a difference in your life before and after doing the changercise?

4. How would you use this changercise to take action on a specific situation you need to change?

Share your changercise with a friend. Each of you can do the changercise and you can communicate with each other about the questions and your answers. You can communicate by text, e-mail, or the old-fashioned way, by phone. I guarantee this will speed up your ability to apply this in your daily life and help you reach your three-sentence goal that much faster.

And then make sure you share it with us at www. changercise.com and keep us in your loop.

This is all about
your choice to change.

Chapter 5
Magic . . .

This changercise is all about that special word . . . magic.

What is *magic*?

David Copperfield defines *magic* as "the art of controlling events by supernatural power."

Harry Houdini became famous for his magic of freeing himself from self-imposed handcuffs and shackles, chains, and ropes of many kinds.

Let's combine the two definitions.

The art of controlling events by supernatural power such as freeing oneself from self-imposed handcuffs and shackles, chains, and ropes of many kinds.

Why do *magic*?

It would be pretty amazing if you could perform such feats like David and Harry are known for on yourself, wouldn't it?

Go to the introduction and read what you wrote as your three-sentence goal for reading this book.

Is it working? Are you getting closer to that goal?

Whether you realize it or not, you are bound by self-imposed handcuffs and shackles, chains, and ropes of many kinds.

So what is the supernatural power you can use to control events and get closer to your definite goals? What is the magic?

One definition of *supernatural* is *hidden power.*

Now, let's look at the definition of magic this way—the art of controlling events by *hidden power* such as freeing oneself from self-imposed handcuffs and shackles, chains, and ropes of many kinds.

This *hidden power* is the magic you already possess.

Are you ready to break free from your self-imposed bonds?

Okay, let's do it!

How to do *magic.*

Doing magic, your *hidden power,* is based on one simple three-letter word. I have alluded to it throughout the various changercises you've been doing.

The three-letter word is *why*.

You need what Napoleon Hill called *a definiteness of purpose*. It is that hidden power, the magic of *why* that so many successful people use.

The crazy thing is that it's not really hidden at all. It is there for all to see. It is there for all to tap into. It is your choice. So . . .

Let's do *magic*.

This final changercise will require some real digging. And I mean digging deep.

This changercise will take from thirty minutes to an hour or two . . . your choice. You will need a tablet, computer, or pen and paper.

You may want total silence, or you may want the music you love to listen to when you want to be inspired. You may want to sit at a table, or you may want to lie down. You may want to be inside your home, or you may want to be outside.

So let's get going.

Here are the questions I asked you in chapter 1. Now, please answer them again here . . .

I want you to answer the following sentences in this order:

Five years ago . . .
Who was I?

Who did I want to be?

Ten years ago . . .
Who was I?

Who did I want to be?

Fifteen years ago . . .
Who was I?

Who did I want to be?

In high school . . .
Who was I?

Who did I want to be?

As a ten-year-old . . .
Who was I?

Who did I want to be?

Today, here and now . . .
Who am I?

What was my vision of where I would be today?

What's different?

What works?

What doesn't?

What must change?

Today, here and now . . .
What have I done, and been?

What do I feel great about?

Today, here and now . . .
What do I regret not doing?

What do I regret not being?

Today, here and now . . .
What do I want to do even if I don't think I can?

What do I want to be even if I don't think I can?

Today, here and now . . .
What would I do if I knew I couldn't fail?

What would I be if I knew I couldn't fail?

Who do you want to become?

How has that changed?

What's the dream now?

What must change?

What steps do you need to take today to change your direction?

That was hard work wasn't it? You should be proud of yourself for digging deep to find these answers. Well done!

Okay, now that you have answered these questions for the second time, see how they compare to your previous answers in chapter 1.

Are the answers the same or are they different?

Have you changed your outlook on yourself?

Have you changed your beliefs in your abilities?

Have you changed what you want to achieve?

Have you already started making changes?

Okay. Now stop writing and ask yourself . . .
What are you waiting *four*?

Yes, I wrote *four* because there is a very wise saying from Robert Schuller: "If it's going to be, it's up *to me*."

And most people use these four letters, T O M E, as the four reasons/excuses they don't achieve their goals.

<u>T</u>ime
<u>O</u>pportunity
<u>M</u>oney
<u>E</u>ducation

Did you find the one you're using?
If you dig deep enough, you will.

Journal your response.

This reminds me of the story about the five frogs sitting on a log in the forest. Four decide to jump off. How many are left? I'll give the math wizards a moment on this. Okay, the answer is one, right? *Wrong*! The answer is *five*. They only *decided* to jump. They never actually jumped. They took no real action.

Achieving results requires thoughts, feelings, and real *action*.

Remember, your actual *magic* (the hidden power you have) is your *why*. You need to make your *why* so strong that it no longer is a need or want—it becomes a <u>M</u> <u>U</u> <u>S</u> <u>T</u>: <u>m</u>akes <u>u</u> <u>s</u>tay <u>t</u>argeted.

Think back to a time in your life that something was a <u>M</u> <u>U</u> <u>S</u> <u>T</u>! Did you get it done? Was it easy, or at that time did that not even matter? Easy or difficult, you still got it accomplished. Maybe not in the time frame you wanted, but you still eventually succeeded in getting it done. You had made your *why* a <u>M</u> <u>U</u> <u>S</u> <u>T</u>, whether you were aware of it or not.

Journal your thoughts.

The one thing that successful people clearly have in common is that their *why* becomes a <u>M</u> <u>U</u> <u>S</u> <u>T</u> (<u>m</u>akes <u>u</u> <u>s</u>tay <u>t</u>argeted).

How do you make your *why* (*magic hidden power*) into a <u>M</u> <u>U</u> <u>S</u> <u>T</u>? You make it a no-turning-back moment.

There are many ways to do this.

Here are a few examples from my clients who have gone on to do what they <u>M</u> <u>U</u> <u>S</u> <u>T</u> and be who they <u>M</u> <u>U</u> <u>S</u> <u>T</u>.

They encourage you to take these actions on a daily basis. Many of my clients did these as many as three times a day or more.

- Listen to music that inspires you.

- Do the Who's Laughing Now changercise often.

- Create a visual representation of your <u>M</u> <u>U</u> <u>S</u> <u>T</u>, and put it where you will look at it frequently: in your car, truck, bathroom, kitchen, office, screensaver, workstation, locker, wallet, purse, bedroom, garage, phone, briefcase, lunch box, or anywhere else you can think of.

- Put yourself in your M U S T with all five senses for at least two minutes.

- Create a single sentence that describes your M U S T and say it out loud to yourself, often.

- Act as if you have already become and done your M U S T. Be an actor and assume the part.

- Tell your best friend to start treating you like you have achieved being and doing your M U S T.

- Read a true story that inspires you. (I personally recommend the book *Unstoppable* by Cynthia Kersey to all my clients, past and present.)

- Have a word or phrase you can say to yourself when things don't go as you would have wanted, which helps you to remember *this is just a small bump in the road* toward your M U S T. Here are a few examples:

  - I'm getting closer.
  - This is an opportunity, not a problem.
  - It's just around the corner.
  - That's one more *no* out of the way.
  - All successful people fail first.

So . . .
What are you waiting four . . .

Don't let <u>T</u>ime, <u>O</u>pportunity, <u>M</u>oney, or <u>E</u>ducation be your reasons/excuses for not fulfilling your <u>M</u>akes <u>U</u> <u>S</u>tay <u>T</u>argeted.

Go to www.changercise.com to give us your creative ideas.

Josephine H.

When I was five, I remember watching *The Nutcracker* on TV and deciding I wanted to be a ballerina.

At thirteen, I saw it live. The ballerina seemed to float across the stage as if she were almost flying.

At eighteen, I had forgotten about *almost flying*.

I was set on going to medical school to become a pediatrician.

Fast-forward to present time. I've been in practice for five years.

It's December 15. It is snowing. Nancy, a seven-year-old, comes into my office with her mom. I tell them Nancy will be fine and not to worry; she just has a minor ankle sprain.

I put a wrap on it.

Nancy seems upset. Nancy tells me it happened during ballet practice and she starts to cry. She says she is afraid she will never dance again. I assure her that is not true.

Nancy stops crying and starts to smile.

It's December 23. Nancy keeps popping up in my thoughts. I ignore it. I get home, having fought the holiday traffic, I am exhausted. My husband and I decide to watch a movie on TV.

I surf the TV guide and stumble on *The Nutcracker* on PBS. Watching it, I begin to think of Nancy. Before I know it, I am crying. It only lasts for thirty seconds and goes away. It seems very peculiar, but I ignore it.

It's December 24. (The office is closed for the holidays.) I get out of bed and go downstairs to my study.

I look at notes I took during our client conversations and happen to look at a changercise. It's the one you simply call *Magic* . . . I read the myriad of questions that go with this changercise and think back to my childhood. I then recognize the significance of Nancy.

After a few self-diggings, I realize why I cried. I still want to be a ballerina. I try to give myself excuses/reasons why that dream is dead.

I decide to look at your TOME idea.

I fill in the answers mentally.

Time—I have a busy life and heavy patient load.

Opportunity—I don't know the right people.

Money—It will take a lot of money to do it.

Education—I've never taken a dance class.

Extra bonus excuse/reason:

Age—I am way *too old* to start learning now.

After more self-digging I thought about how I became a doctor.

Without realizing it, I had decided that this would be my *why,* and I made it a M U S T. And with a lot of hard work, I became who I wanted to be, a pediatrician.

Then I asked myself, *What was to stop me from applying this same attitude and philosophy now?*

Me.

Then I thought back to last night and the tears of my inner child trying to resurface.

I M U S T figure this out.

I did what you always recommend. I asked myself, *What are you waiting 'four'?* I looked at the bracelet you ask all your clients to wear and read it out loud to myself. *Change the way you think and think the way to change.*

I decided I had to figure out what thinking had to change.

After thirty days of reading that bracelet, sometimes three times a day, I had my answer.

I knew I had to stop thinking why I *couldn't* reach my goal and start thinking how I *would* reach my goal.

I knew what I M U S T do next.

1. I bought the book you recommend, *Unstoppable*, off your website. I read it for fifteen minutes every evening.

2. I made an mp3 of Tchaikovsky music from ballet and listened to it twice daily.

3. I told my husband everything; he was so supportive.

4. I printed out pictures from the web and made collages of ballerinas. I put them in locations in my home and office.

5. I called around town until I found a ballet teacher who took an "older" student.

6. I found money for classes by selling "stuff" I had in my basement on eBay.

7. I researched the time it would take to learn to do *The Nutcracker* at amateur level. I determined it was four years, the same amount of time it took to get through medical school. I could do it.

8. I started taking ballet classes.

9. I made it my M U S T!

10 I looked at the bracelet every time I felt frustrated and reminded myself I could *change the way I think and think the way to change.*

That was six years ago. About nine months ago, I wrapped up a local production of *The Nutcracker* here in my hometown. Not only was I the lead, but in order to make it happen, I also became the producer. *I knew if it was going to be, it was up to me.*

Many of my patients and parents came to see it, which was a joy and honor for me.

I was so excited to cast Nancy as a dancing snowflake.

By the way, I am pregnant with a baby girl.

I am looking forward to helping her make *her* dreams, whatever they might be, a reality.

And thanks, DW, for the bracelet.

I still wear it and read it at least twice daily.

Let's look at a couple of things Josepine H. learned about change.

She learned that you are never too old to change.

She became clearly focused on a new goal and created definite action steps to achieve it.

She learned how to use the magic of her hidden power, her *why*.

She learned the importance of making her why her M U S T.

She experienced the joy and fulfillment of her dream.

She became very clear on the value of reading the "change the way you think" bracelet daily.

Go to www.changercise.com for other readers' examples and to give us your creative ideas.

Here is *my* why.

I want to share a poem I wrote in 1999 that was inspired by some of the words in Nelson Mandela's inaugural address as he became president of a democratic South Africa in 1994 after being in captivity for twenty-seven years in a South African prison.

You Are the Greatest!

There is no one like you. It is time to admit that.
By not doing so, you are cheating yourself, the world.

You are here to do great works—and you know it.

You are a child of God.

Ever since you were young you knew you were here for a purpose.

And you let the world shrink you down. This is your time.

It is time for you to shine. Your light is a beacon for others to see.

A beacon that illuminates a world of possibilities.

You owe it to the young child within you,

To find your dream again and make it real, now!

Life moves on. Time is short. Not to do so would be a crime.

A crime against you, a crime against humanity.

The world awaits your special gifts and talents, now.

It wants them. It needs them. And only you can deliver them.

To take the challenge to live your dream again is to say to the world—

I am the greatest and so are you. To say to the world, here's my hand—

Join me as together we live our lives on purpose.

DW Starr

You can purchase my poem in many forms at my website.

Go to www.changercise.com to give us your creative magic ideas.

Clients' comments about this changercise:

- "As a pretty successful salesperson I have always known about the magic of *why*. But now I understand how the <u>M</u> <u>U</u> <u>S</u> <u>T</u> is interwoven with it. The two together are unstoppable. By the way, I bought that book from your website. It's great."

- "This changercise helped me understand the reason certain projects at work never seem to get finished. I even started teaching some of my team from the notes I took when I was a client of yours."

- "This changercise was really hard for me. It took some major digging to admit to myself I wasn't clear on my *why*. I'm still in that process, but I want you to know it's worth the effort. I've already seen some positive effects with my kids."

It's time to figure out what you learned and how you can apply it to your daily/weekly/monthly work and personal life and share with other readers if you choose.

Either by using paper or your favorite electronic device, journaling these answers will help you reach your original three-sentence goal you jotted down at the very beginning of this process, in the introduction. Write out the answer to each question with thoughtful consideration.

1. How would you describe the magic of *why* to a friend?

2. What have you decided is your most important M U S T?

3. What obstacles are still in your way from making your *why* your M U S T?

4. How would you use this changercise to take action on a specific situation you need to change?

Share your changercise with a friend. Each of you can do the changercise and you can communicate with each other about the questions and your answers. You can communicate by text, e-mail, or the old-fashioned way, by phone. I guarantee this will speed up your ability to apply this in your daily life and help you reach your three-sentence goal that much faster.

And then make sure you share it with us at www. changercise.com and keep us in your loop.

> *This is all about*
> *your choice to change.*

Originally, this was going to be the last chapter of changercise.

I've decided to add a bonus chapter.

You can get very creative with this one.

Have fun with it!

Bonus Chapter
Opposite Hand Attack

I find this changercise to be very revealing as well as giving you plenty of opportunity for fresh brain creativity.

It's your bonus changercise.

I use this changercise in my life every day. In fact, I use it many times a day.

More Changercises, my second book, is being written as you read this one. So if you have an idea for a changercise to include in it, please send it to me at my website.

What is *Opposite Hand Attack*?

I will start by calling the hand you use the most often your dominant hand (DH) and the one you use less your nondominant hand (NDH). By the way, this changercise is called *Opposite Hand Attack* because that sounds a lot cooler than nondominant hand focusing. Wouldn't you agree? I hope so. Anyway, what we are going to do for today is use your NDH to do something that is very common to you on a daily basis. I'll give you three examples. You can do one, two, or all three. It's your choice.

Why do Opposite Hand Attack?

The key reason to do Opposite Hand Attack is to keep your brain functioning at its peak.

When you do your routines with your DH such as brush your teeth, pour your coffee, use your microwave, or write your name, you are using the same neural networks over and over again. The results are a life of predictability. It's almost as if you do these routines at a subconscious level.

You are not giving your brain change.

So when you say you could probably drive to work with your eyes closed, you are closer to the truth than you might think.

By using your NDH, you create new neural pathways that stimulate mental growth.

When you do the same things over and over, year after year, you get to a point somewhere in your life that it becomes the only way you do a particular action. In fact, you believe that it is the only way you are *able* to do that particular action.

This changercise is designed to change that concept and move you in the direction of belief in your fuller brain potential.

How to do Opposite Hand Attack.

Go get a pen. Put the pen in your DH. Now, for most of the world, that would be their right hand. For those of you whose DH is your left hand, I want you to know that this changercise may be a bit easier for you than for the right-handed folks.

Now take the pen and put it in your NDH, hence the title Opposite Hand Attack.

With the pen in your NDH, I want you to write your name on the line below

_____

Pretty simple technique, huh?

Remember what Einstein said about simplicity. (Read the introduction if you didn't already.)

Did you *write* it as I asked you to, or did you *print* it like most people often do?

Okay, now that you are familiar with OHA (Opposite Hand Attack), I am going to ask you to do something that will seem strange to you at first. Go to the bathroom where you get ready in the morning.

Before I continue, let me explain the three levels I will be referring to in this chapter.

Each level contains specific movements you will make with your NDH. The first level is the most basic and contains few movements.

The second level contains more movements and requires more dexterity.

The third level has the most complex movements and requires the most dexterity.

The more complex the level, the more self-confidence you will build in your ability to do new things and change; you will also create more new neural pathways, which will enhance your brain growth. This enhances your ability to *change the way you think and think the way to change.*

First, you are going to use an example from level 1: *brushing your teeth.*

The first step is to brush your teeth the way you normally do, with the hand that you normally use, your dominant hand (DH). At this point, I want you to pay attention to all the minor details involved in doing.

Pretend as if you will have to teach someone who has never brushed his or her teeth before. Put the toothpaste on the way you normally do. Turn the water on with the hand you normally use.

How do you hold the brush? How do you put the brush back to where you keep it? Remember, pay attention to every little detail as if you were going to teach it to someone. If you choose, you can take notes.

If you are like me, you probably had no idea how many little moves it takes to do something as everyday as brushing your teeth.

So now you're done; the brush is put away, the water is off, the towel is hung up, the cabinet or drawer is closed, the cup is put away, and you are now standing outside of your bathroom.

Congratulations! You have successfully paid attention and given awareness to something you have been doing since you were three years old, or maybe even younger. Now take a five-minute break.

Okay, you're back outside the bathroom. Now comes the fun and the challenge. From this minute forward, for at least five minutes, I want you to use your nondominant hand (NDH).

Start out simply and slowly. You can get more complex and faster later with practice. If you took notes, now would be a good time to refer to them.

Change the way you think and think the way to change.

So that means for at least five minutes you are only allowed to use your NDH to hold the brush or the tube of toothpaste.

Under no circumstances are you to revert back to your normal use of your DH. You would turn on the water with your NDH. And you would also rinse your mouth by holding the cup of water with your NDH.

At first this will seem silly and maybe even ridiculous—picking up and putting down the brush so many times. You also may end up making a lot of extra moves that seem unnecessary. Press on!

Einstein said, "For an idea which at first does not seem absurd there is no hope."

As you may have already noticed, many actions are done by both your NDH and your DH. Your goal is to do as much as you can in the time span you have selected with your focus on your NDH.

So of course you need to use your DH as a supportive resource. Normally that would be with your NDH. In essence you are switching the two. Was it easier or harder than you expected?

For your second example, let's use another level 1 example: *pouring and drinking your coffee in the morning.* As in the first example, you will need to do it the first time the way you normally would.

Now this will be a challenge, so you might want to just drink half your normal amount on the first half of this example; otherwise, you'll have to drink twice the normal amount, in which case you may speed through the second half of the changercise. Just kidding!

Pay strict attention to the use of both hands, in this case, especially the NDH. You will probably be surprised at how little you use it. Take notes if you choose.

Once you've either finished the cup (or half the cup), walk away for five minutes.

Okay, you're back.

Now let's look at what it might look like when you use your NDH.

Once the coffee has brewed, you would take the coffee cup in your NDH and place it on the counter. Then you would pick up the coffee pot and pour it in the cup with your NDH.

Now if you want creamer and/or sugar, you would go to the cabinet where the sugar is and open it with you NDH and take out the sugar bowl with your NDH. Then you would pick up the spoon and put the sugar in the cup with your NDH.

Now for the creamer, you would open the refrigerator with your NDH and take out the creamer. You would open the creamer with your NDH and pour it into the cup with your NDH.

And for both the sugar and creamer you would return them to their respective locations when you are done with them with your NDH. Now doing this will probably take a few extra steps that would ordinarily not be needed.

Remember, this is important to the changercise.

Okay, it's now time for you to pour and drink your coffee with your NDH.

How did it go this time? Was it easier or harder than you expected?

Let's use for your third example another from level 1, *using your microwave.*

So as done previously, heat or reheat something with your DH as you would normally do it.

You may even want to include the example *getting food out of the refrigerator.*

Pay strict attention to each detail of the use of both your hands, noting which hand is doing which action. Again, you can take notes if you choose.

Now I will admit that at first glance this seems very basic, even childish at first. Make no mistake about it; this is in no way childish. This is helping you to get a clearer perception of what you currently take for granted.

Once you have taken the action with your DH, take a five-minute break.

Okay, your break is over and you are ready to do this changercise with your NDH.

This one will seem easy at first, but watch how you quickly forget somewhere in the middle of this changercise and either use your NDH in the wrong sequence or use your DH in place of your NDH. It happens to many people the first few times.

So now you know how to use your NDH for a level 1 changercise.

For a level 2 or 3 changercise, it will get increasingly more challenging to do them. They also take more discipline, practice, and self-observation.

The three levels of changercise and their corresponding examples are listed at the end of this chapter.

Change the way you think and think the way to change.

I keep using this phrase. I do so to remind you that when you approach an opportunity with the same level of thinking that created it, you are sure to get the same result over and over again. That is just like using your DH to the point of predictability. By changing the way you think about an opportunity, you are more likely to get a different result, because you are using newly created neural pathways.

Maryanne D.

I work as one of ten secretaries in the corporate offices of a very large bank.

Being right-handed, I put the pen in my left hand (NDH) and proceeded to print my name.

I felt like I should have done better, even though it was a first attempt.

I decided right then and there that I would do this changercise once a week as DW suggested, since he said it would help me with my creativity and decision-making at work.

I also kept the original sheet of paper as a way to compare my *change* in the future.

After six weeks, I found that my writing with my NDH was just as neat, or neater than with my DH. I believe that practice and focus made a big difference. I was slowly changing.

I decided to text with my best friend, Cheryl, about my process—both my thoughts and feelings, as DW suggested.

By the third week, with Cheryl's encouragement, I decided I would use Opposite Hand Attack (OHA) to tie my running shoes with my NDH. Now, talk about a challenge.

That is when I noticed how much I actually use both hands for very different tasks. Using my NDH was very difficult.

Each week I would text Cheryl my notes. This may seem like a trivial pursuit and even a waste of time, but it's not.

And after eight weeks of struggling I was finally able to do it. Not only was the NDH accomplishment fulfilling, I learned some important lessons about myself and others.

Deciding to and then taking action to *change* is contagious and inspiring. By the third week of texting about my shoe-tying experiences, Cheryl wanted to give it a shot too! And she did!

I learned that I could do something that a few months earlier I would have never thought I could do. So after I mastered that changercise, I decided to sit down with myself and really look at the self-imposed limits I had been carrying around for so long. What else could I do that I was holding myself back from?

My confidence began to build as I tried out and succeeded at doing a few different OHAs. As I continued to build new neural pathways, as you said I would, I found that at work I was coming up with more creative solutions to some of the problems I was facing.

I increasingly found my attitude about my capabilities rubbing off at work, as well. I was taking on new challenges, without being asked to. That gave me more confidence to try more OHA examples from level 2 and eventually level 3.

By the time I was able to shave my legs and underarms (without nicking myself) and had four months of practice, I knew I had built up enough self-confidence to ask for a raise.

My boss said that it was clear something about me had changed. My boss said I was making better choices, contributing more to the team, and I deserved a raise. That was a really big deal for me. It really got me thinking in a new direction.

I decided by expanding my belief in myself, by doing these changercises, I could be a manager someday. (This had always been a dream of mine that I would keep pushing away due to my self-doubts.)

Six months later, this changercise program has really helped me get a much clearer look at my true potential. And now, since I've been doing many of the other changercises, I am able to take on even more challenges and am thinking even clearer in my work choices and decisions.

(More neural pathways created.)

I'm so excited—*I've been asked by my boss if I want to join the management training program.*

I recommend you try these changercises for yourself and find out what they can do for you.

Let's look at a couple of things Maryanne D. learned about change.

Getting the support of a coworker or friend is very helpful when making a change.

Using her NDH, she learned a valuable lifelong lesson, which was that she did not have to live by her self-imposed limits.

She learned that she was worthy of being a manager and could stretch herself to be one.

She found that doing this changercise opened up her neural pathways to more creativity and better decision-making. Who wouldn't want that in their work or personal life?

At first look, before doing this changercise, it may only seem like it provides a way to be able to use either hand to do something you thought you could only do with your DH.

After you did the changercise, did you have any of these thoughts?

- Did I print instead of write because that was a way to take the easy way out so it would end up at least looking decent? It's always harder in the beginning.

- Do I set my standards too high, too soon? Familiarity breeds *comfortability* and then skill. Some things always seem harder than they actually are.

- If I can do this, what else can I do? I am what I am capable of, not just what I'm doing. I thought and truly believed I was right-/left-handed my whole life. That's been my NDH since I was a baby. I am not what I do; I am who I am.

- If I can do this, that means I could have done it all along.

Below are three levels of complexity for Opposite Hand Attack. The levels are based on the quantity of actions and focused thinking involved in the examples.

Level 1

- printing your name with a pen

- setting your alarm clock two hours later

- brushing your teeth

- combing/brushing your hair

- eating your favorite snack

- making a phone call

- texting a friend

- blowing your nose

- using your microwave

- opening a car or office door

- getting food out of the refrigerator

- putting on socks or underwear

- putting your shoes on

- pouring/drinking a cup of coffee

Level 2

- signing your name

- jotting a quick note

- vacuuming or sweeping

- brushing your dog or cat

- writing a work e-mail

- eating an entire meal

Level 3

- shaving your face or legs

- tying your shoes

- tying a tie or scarf

- backing up on your driveway

- putting on your makeup

Go to www.changercise.com to give us your creative ideas and levels and to see other readers' ideas and levels.

Below are suggestions from my clients of variations to Opposite Hand Attack with one of many potential ways to do each one:

Variations on OHA

Opposite Wrist Attack
Putting your watch on it

Opposite Foot Attack
Kicking a ball with it

Opposite Leg Attack
Start out walking with opposite leg

Opposite Ear Attack
Listening to music with just one ear

Opposite Eye Attack
Looking at an object with just one eye

Opposite Hand-Gesture Attack
Saluting or waving with a hand gesture

Opposite Driving-Direction Attack
Changing the route you take to work or home

Go to www.changercise.com for other readers' examples and to give us your variation ideas.

Clients' comments about this changercise:

- "I like that it was easy to do because I could do it anywhere, anytime."

- "I was amazed at how such a simple changercise could bring about so much change in how I think about my abilities now. I've really started making some major moves toward a new position in the company."

- "I love how this changercise has opened up my creativity in ways I would never have imagined. I have taken on new projects that just six months ago, I would have never believed possible."

It's time to figure out what you learned and how you can apply it to your daily/weekly/monthly work and personal life and *share with other readers if you choose.*

Either by using paper or your favorite electronic device, journaling these answers will help you reach your original three-sentence goal you jotted down at the very beginning of this process, in the introduction. Write out the answer to each question with thoughtful consideration.

1. What were some of your different thoughts/feelings/observations as you did something as common as *brushing your teeth* when you were using your DH/NDH?

2. How did the changercise help you be more creative? (new neural pathways created)

3. What did you learn about your own self-concept and limiting beliefs?

4. How would you use this changercise to take action on a specific situation you need to change?

Share your changercise with a friend. Each of you can do the changercise and you can communicate with each other about the questions and your answers. You can communicate by text, e-mail, or the old-fashioned way, by phone. I guarantee this will speed up your ability to apply this in your daily life and help you reach your three-sentence goal that much faster.

And then make sure you share it with us at www. changercise.com and keep us in your loop.

*This is all about
your choice to change.*

Conclusion
Is This the Final Chapter?

Here is what I said in the book's introduction:

Changercise is designed to be your living change manual. Although each of the five changercises (plus the bonus changercise) is independent of the others, when used together, they create exponential change. *Changercise* can be used in many ways. You can read it like any other book, page by page or chapter by chapter. You can skip to a favorite chapter, or for some of you, the final chapter. You can skim the italicized words to get the gist. You can use it to only do the assignments at the end of each chapter. It's your choice.

Throughout *Changercise*, I have set out to help you see the power, value, and normalcy of change. Even the mention of the word *change* sends shivers down many people's spines. It needn't be that way.

Key Points

- Change is a constant. You can see change as an adversary or as a friend. *It is your choice.*

- Assessing where and who you wanted to be from an earlier perspective helps you clarify how you see yourself today—and where and who you see yourself being tomorrow.

- There are various ways to create your own quiet time.

- Silence is a tool for better mental well-being. It acts as both a calmer and energizer at the same time. Bringing it back into your routine creates stability.

- Our past can be a place of great joy, sadness, or both.

- Examining how we reacted and responded to situations and people in the past can provide a clearer path for growth today.

- Without us even realizing it, we develop lifelong learning patterns. These patterns affect our adult lives in so many ways.

- Use your dominant sense to re-create the memory of an event.

- Pattern repetition is a very common cause of the fear of change. Learning to recognize the patterns and triggers of the past is the first step in changing them. You can't change what you don't know.

- Different changercises work in tandem, synergistically.

- Creating a baseline for your healthy zone (HZ) is a critical piece of the puzzle.

- No matter how negative the results of being in your OZ might be, you still find positive pieces in your own personal ouch zones, pieces that fill a need of some kind.

- Getting rid of your ouch zones is fun for some, a relief for others.

- Your belief system is based on your past experiences . . . so you anticipate your future being like your past. It's time to live through the eyes of today.

- Sources of laughter are available to you in many forms.

- You can get so busy with work and personal stuff that you shut out *funny time* from your life.

- Humor combats fear. Humor comforts. Humor relaxes. Humor reduces pain. Humor boosts the immune system. Humor reduces stress. Humor helps in communication. Humor often spreads happiness.

- Whether you realize it or not, you are bound by self-imposed handcuffs and shackles, chains, and ropes of many kinds.

- *Magic*, the hidden power you possess, is your *why*!

- <u>T</u>ime, <u>O</u>pportunity, <u>M</u>oney, <u>E</u>ducation—Which one are *you* using as your excuse/reason for not reaching your goals? You may have to dig deep to find it.

- A decision by itself is not enough. It needs real action to achieve results.

- Make your *why* a <u>M</u> <u>U</u> <u>S</u> <u>T</u>!

- It becomes your no-turning-back moment.

Bonus Chapter
Quick Key Points

- You do not have to live by your self-imposed limits.
- Creating new neural pathways stimulates more creativity and better decision-making.

- Sometimes you set your standards too high too soon.
- OHA can be done almost anywhere at any time.
- OHA is fun and great for creating new neural pathways and mental creativity.

So there you have it—five changercises plus a bonus that can help you make major changes in your life if you let them.

I want to hear from you. I want to know how this book is helping you. *Please contact me.*

Send me your e-mails, or post your thoughts and ideas at www.changercise.com.

Keep me in your loop, and I'll keep you in mine.

I will leave you with the words I say so often in my workshops and when I speak to audiences: *Change is the essence of life. Be willing to surrender who you are for who you will become.*

Until we meet, which I hope will be real soon, thank you for letting me share with you and for investing time and energy in yourself.

Go be the change
you know you can be!

Keep on Changin'!

References

Here is a list of some of the references my clients and I have read over the years that have helped inspire us to be and do our <u>M</u> <u>U</u> <u>S</u> <u>T</u>.

There is a quick summary of many of these references on my website, where they can also be purchased.

Go to www.changercise.com.

Here are my top ten favorites:

Cosby, Bill. *Fatherhood.*
Dyer, Wayne. *The Sky's the Limit.*
Frankl, Viktor. *Man's Search for Meaning.*
Hill, Napoleon. *Think and Grow Rich.*
Kersey, Cynthia. *Unstoppable.*
Newberry, Tommy. *Success Is No Accident.*
Ryan, M. J. *Attitudes of Gratitude.*
Schwartz, David. *The Magic of Thinking Big.*
Tough, Paul. *How Children Succeed.*
Wiseman, Richard. *The Luck Factor.*

Here are others in alphabetical order by author:

Berne, Eric. *Games People Play.*
Blanchard, Ken and Sheldon Bowles. *Gung Ho!*

Blanchard, Ken, and Spencer Johnson. *The One Minute Manager.*

Brafman, Rom. *Succeeding When You're Supposed to Fail.*

Burchard, Brendon. *Charge.*

Byrne, Rhonda. *The Secret.*

Canfield, Jack, Mark Hansen, and Bud Gardner. *Chicken Soup for the Writer's Soul.*

Carnegie, Dale. *How to Win Friends and Influence People.*

Chopra, Deepak. *The Seven Spiritual Laws of Success.*

Coburn, Pip. *The Change Function.*

Cousins, Norman. 1979. http://laughterheals.org/articles.php.

Covey, Sean. *The Seven Habits of Highly Effective Teens.*

Curtis, Bryan. *Classic Wisdom for the Good Life.*

Dispenza, Joe. *Evolve Your Brain.*

Duhigg, Charles. *The Power of Habit.*

Dyer, Wayne. *The Power of Intention.*

Eker, T. Harv. *Secrets of the Millionaire Mind.*

Fast Company magazine.

Ferriss, Timothy. *The 4-Hour Workweek.*

Frank, Milo. *How to Get Your Point Across in 30 Seconds or Less.*

Gitomer, Jeffrey. *Little Gold Book of Yes! Attitude.*

Gitomer, Jeffrey. *The Little Platinum Book of Cha-Ching!*

Gitomer, Jeffrey. *The Little Red Book of Selling.*

Gladwell, Malcolm. *Blink.*

Gladwell, Malcolm. *Outliers.*

Gladwell, Malcolm. *The Tipping Point.*

Gladwell, Malcolm. *What the Dog Saw.*

Godek, Gregory. *1001 Ways to Be Romantic.*

Gordon, David, and Graham Dawes. *Expanding Your World.*

Gray, John. *Men Are from Mars, Women Are from Venus.*

Great Quotations Publishing. *Cornerstones of Success.*

Harvard Business School Publishing. *Managing Time.*

Hawking, Stephen. *A Stubbornly Persistent Illusion.*

Hopkins, Tom. *Selling for Dummies.*

Humor and Health Journal.

Inc. magazine.

Isaacson, Walter. *Einstein.*

Johnson, Spencer, and Larry Wilson. *The One Minute Sales Person.*

Kahneman, Daniel. *Thinking, Fast and Slow.*

Katz, Lawrence. *Keep Your Brain Alive.*

Klein, Allen. *The Celebrate-Your-Life Quote Book.*

Lewis, Michael. *Boomerang.*

Mandino, Og. *The Greatest Miracle in the World.*

Mandino, Og. *The Greatest Salesman in the World.*

The Masters of Success by Insight Publishing.

Peale, Norman Vincent. *The Amazing Results of Positive Thinking.*

Peck, Scott M. *The Road Less Travelled.*

Pink, Daniel. *Drive.*

Popcorn, Faith. *Dictionary of the Future.*

Psychology Today magazine.

Raskin, Victor, ed. *The Primer of Humor Research.*

Richardson, Pam. *The Life Coach.*

Robbins, Anthony. *Awaken the Giant Within.*

Rumbauskas, Frank Jr. *Selling Sucks.*

Schuller, Robert. *Self Love.*

Schwartz, David. *The Magic of Self Direction.*

Simon, David. *The Ten Commitments.*

Skerrett, P. J. "Laugh and be thankful—it's good for the heart." *Harvard Health Blog.*

Stutz, Phil, and Barry Michels. *The Tools.*

Tan, Stanley, and Lee Berk. *Loma Linda University Study on Neuroimmune Parameters.*

Thaler, Richard, and Cass Sunstein. *Nudge.*

Traynor, Dave. "American Fitness." *Journal of Holistic Nursing.*

Tucker, Toni, and Judith Adler. *Zen Dog.*

Von Oech, Roger. *A Wack on the Side of the Head.*

Walters, Dottie, and Lilly Walters. *Speak and Grow Rich.*

Weber, Alan. *Rules of Thumb.*

Weinman Lear, Martha. *Where Did I Leave My Glasses?*

Wilkinson, Bruce. *The Dream Giver.*

www.TED.com/talks.

Zadra, Dan, and Katie Lambert. *Because of You.*

Go to www.changercise.com for other readers' reference favorites and to give us yours.